MONSON
Free Library and Reading Room
ASSOCIATION

NO.

62222

RULES AND REGULATIONS

Assessed fines shall be paid by every person keeping Library materials beyond the specified time.

Every person who borrows Library materials shall be responsible for all loss or damage to same while they are out in his name.

All library materials shall be returned to the Library on the call of the Librarian or Directors.

General Laws of Mass., Chap. 266, Sec. 99

Whoever willfully and maliciously or wantonly and without cause writes upon, injures, defaces, tears or destroys a book, plate, picture, engraving or statute belonging to a law, town, city or other public library shall be punished by a fine of not less than five nor more than fifty dollars, or by imprisonment in the jail not exceeding six months.

Modern Critical Interpretations

Virgil's
Aeneid

Modern Critical Interpretations

These and other titles in preparation

Virgil's

Aeneid

Edited and with an introduction by
Harold Bloom
Sterling Professor of the Humanities
Yale University

Chelsea House Publishers ◊ *1987*
NEW YORK ◊ NEW HAVEN ◊ PHILADELPHIA

Library of Congress Cataloging-in-Publication Data
Virgil's The Aeneid.
    (Modern critical interpretations)
    Bibliography: p.
    Includes index.
    Summary: A collection of six critical essays on
Virgil's epic poem, arranged in chronological order
of original publication.
    1. Virgil. Aeneid.   2. Aeneas (Legendary character)
in literature.   [1. Virgil. Aeneid.   2. Aeneas
(Legendary character) in literature.   3. Classical
literature—History and criticism]   I. Bloom,
Harold,   II. Series.
PA6825.V5   1987   873'.01   86–29957
ISBN 0–87754–919–2 (alk. paper)

Contents

Editor's Note

This book brings together a representative selection of the most useful criticism available of Virgil's *Aeneid*. The critical essays are arranged here in the chronological order of their original publication. I am grateful to Marena Fisher for her aid in editing this volume.

My introduction meditates upon Virgil's poetic originality, which I see as centered in his peculiar gift of negative imagination. The chronological sequence begins with Viktor Pöschl, who sees the hero Aeneas "as a man of memory and of inner vision." Thomas Greene, studying Virgil's style, emphasizes "the moral ambivalence which personality entails" throughout the *Aeneid*. Greene's insights are cognate with Adam Parry's distinction between the poem's two dominant voices, Augustan and elegiac.

W. R. Johnson, whose *Darkness Visible* may be the best critical study of Virgil, studies the contrast between the poem's surfaces, which shine with bright images of illusion, and its depths, which figure the terrible reality of the will of Juno. In an exegesis of the Dido episode, Barbara J. Bono sees it as exposing an intensity of longing for a spiritual vision more comforting than any Virgil could hope to know.

In this book's final essay, K. W. Gransden insists that "for Virgil all war is mad and one cannot conduct oneself morally on the battlefield." Gransden, like Johnson and Bono, takes us back full circle to this book's introduction, itself heavily influenced by Johnson, and to our contemporary view of Virgil as an ancestor of our nightmare discontents, our nostalgias, and our fitful hopes for what yet might be.

Introduction

When Aeneas is sent by Virgil to the shades, he meets Dido the Queen of Carthage, whom his perfidy had hurried to the grave; he accosts her with tenderness and excuses; but the lady turns away like Ajax in mute disdain. She turns away like Ajax, but she resembles him in none of those qualities which give either dignity or propriety to silence. She might, without any departure from the tenour of her conduct, have burst out like other injured women into clamour, reproach, and denunciation; but Virgil had his imagination full of Ajax, and therefore could not prevail on himself to teach Dido any other mode of resentment.
—DR. SAMUEL JOHNSON, *The Rambler,* no. 121

I

To be employed as the key instance of "the dangers of imitation" by the greatest Western literary critic is the saddest of all Virgil's melancholy-ridden posthumous vicissitudes. It is unhappy enough that the excessively noble Aeneas should be considered by many readers to be a prig, a Trojan version of George Eliot's Daniel Deronda, as it were. But to read Virgil while keeping Homer too steadily in mind is clearly to impose upon the strongest Latin poet a burden that only a few Western writers could sustain. Virgil is not Dante or Shakespeare, Tolstoy or Joyce. He has his affinities with Tennyson, and with other poets in the elegiac mode, down to Matthew Arnold and T. S. Eliot, both of whom celebrated Virgil as a beautiful "inadequacy" (Arnold) and a mature "poet of unique destiny" (Eliot), two apparently antithetical judgments that actually say much the same thing, which is not much. Like Arnold and Eliot, poor Virgil has become the poet of professors, many of whom praise Virgil as a splendid revisionist of Homer, a very different view from Dr. Johnson's.

Other classicists have given us a more Tennysonian Virgil, a knowing latecomer infatuated "with twilight moods, with blurred images, with haunted, half-enacted interviews and confrontations that disintegrate before our eyes just as we begin to perceive them." I quote from *Darkness Visible* by W. R. Johnson, the best study of Virgil that I have

1

read, and hasten to add that Johnson is eloquently summing up the judgment of other critics, rather than stating his own, which seems to me more persuasive. W. R. Johnson's Virgil is marked by a "vast Epicurean sensitivity to pain and suffering," and is not concerned so much "about winning battles but about losing them and learning how to lose them." This Virgil has the "imagination of darkness" and has "discovered and revealed the perennial shape of what truly destroys us."

In some sense, W. R. Johnson moves the fantastic and menacing figure of Virgil's Juno to the center of the epic, which is certainly a useful corrective to many previous readings of Virgil. Juno is Virgil's most ambiguous achievement, and doubtless is one of the major Western representations of what contemporary feminist critics like to call the projection of male hysteria. I would prefer to name Virgil's Juno as the male dread that origin and end will turn out to be one. We do not judge Nietzsche to be hysterical when he warns us, in his *Genealogy of Morals,* that origin and end, for the sake of life, must be kept apart. Despite his all-too-frequently deconstructed dislike of women (so amiable, compared to his master Schopenhauer's), Nietzsche is hardly to be dismissed as what feminists like to call a "patriarchal critic" (are there any? could there be?). What Nietzsche suggests, as Freud does after him, is that all Western images are either origin or end, except for the trope of the father.

It is frightening that the only Western image that is neither origin nor end is, in Virgil, reduced to the pathetic figure of Anchises, who has to be carried out of burning Troy upon the shoulders of his pious son, the drearily heroic Aeneas. The image of the mother in the poem is somehow not that of the merely actual mother, Venus, but rather the hardly maternal Juno, who is truly one of the great nightmare images in Western literary tradition. Virgil is rightly wary of her, and if we read closely, so are we:

> O hateful race, and fate of the Phrygians
> Pitted against my own. Could they be killed
> On the Sigean battlefield? When beaten,
> Could they be beaten? Troy on fire, did Troy
> Consume her men? Amid the spears, amid
> The flames, they found a way. I must, for my part,
> Think my powers by this time tired out,
> Supine, or sleeping, surfeited on hate?
> Well, when they were ejected from their country
> I had the temerity as their enemy

To dog them, fight them, over the whole sea,
These refugees. The strength of sea and sky
Has been poured out against these Teucrians.
What were the Syretës worth to me, or Scylla,
What was huge Charybdis worth? By Tiber's
Longed-for bed they now lay out their town,
Unworried by deep water or by me.
Mars had the power to kill the giant race
Of Lapiths, and the Father of Gods himself
Gave up old Cálydon to Diana's wrath:
And what great sin brought Cálydon or Lapiths
Justice so rough? How differently with me,
The great consort of Jove, who nerved myself
To leave no risk unventured, lent myself
To every indignity. I am defeated
And by Aeneas. Well, if my powers fall short,
I need not falter over asking help
Wherever help may lie. If I can sway
No heavenly hearts I'll rouse the world below.
It will not be permitted me—so be it—
To keep the man from rule in Italy;
By changeless fate Lavinia waits, his bride.
And yet to drag it out, to pile delay
Upon delay in these great matters—that
I can do: to destroy both countries' people,
That I can do. Let father and son-in-law
Unite at that cost to their own! In blood,
Trojan and Latin, comes your dowry, girl;
Bridesmaid Bellona waits now to attend you.
Hecuba's not the only one who carried
A burning brand within her and bore a son
Whose marriage fired a city. So it is
With Venus' child, a Paris once again,
A funeral torch again for Troy reborn!
            (7.295–326, Fitzgerald translation)

There is certainly a dark sense in which Juno is Virgil's pragmatic Muse, as it were, the driving force of his poem. She represents, in this passage, Virgil's authentic if repressed aggressivity towards his daunting father, Homer. As the inspiration of an agonistic intensity, she necessarily speaks for Virgil himself when he confronts the *Iliad* and the *Odyssey*:

> Well, if my powers fall short,
> I need not falter over asking help
> Wherever help may lie. If I can sway
> No heavenly hearts I'll rouse the world below.

Is not that Virgil's actual achievement as compared to Homer's? Juno, though she is a nightmare, is Virgil's own nightmare, his dark creation, a "darkness visible" in the great Miltonic phrase that W. R. Johnson chose as title for his study of the *Aeneid*. What Virgil most powerfully and originally gives us might be called the creatures of Juno: Allecto and the Dira (though technically the Dira is sent by Jupiter). Virgilian invention, though deprecated by Dr. Samuel Johnson, is marked by a negative exuberance that cannot have pleased the author of *Rasselas,* who rightly had his positive imagination full of Homer, and necessarily feared his own dark side.

II

It is no fresh oddity for a poet to become the official representative of the sensibility and ideology of an age, while actually producing work of morbid splendor and equivocal pathology. Virgil's double fate is precisely prophetic of Tennyson's and T. S. Eliot's. Walt Whitman, belatedly accepted as our national bard, would be a parallel figure if his poetry had received wide contemporary acceptance in post-Civil War America, as would Hart Crane, had he been acclaimed in the days of the Depression.

This phenomenon is now over, since our era is overtly paranoid in its sensibility. The best writers in contemporary America—John Ashbery, Thomas Pynchon, James Merrill—are truly representative of the dumbfoundering abyss between the private, aesthetic sensibility and the public sphere of Ronald Reagan. The abyss was as great between Virgil and the Emperor Augustus, but both chose to believe and act otherwise. A vision of President Reagan placing Thomas Pynchon under his patronage is not without its charm.

Virgil, as Dante's precursor, became for Western literary tradition a kind of proto-Christian poet. He can hardly be blamed for this, though perhaps Aeneas can, since Aeneas unfortunately *is* sometimes prophetic of that civic ideal, the Victorian Christian gentleman, Gladstone, say, rather than the exotic Christian Jew, Disraeli. However, Aeneas (though replete with noble sentiments) actually behaves like a cad towards Dido, and finally like a brute towards Turnus. Though no Achilles, Aeneas pragmatically is quite frightening, and really about as benign as the Emperor Augustus, his contemporary model. Machiavelli is more in the line of Aeneas than of Virgil. Perhaps the greatest strength and lasting puzzle of the poem is Virgil's relation to his own hero. Does Virgil, like most of us, prefer Turnus to Aeneas? He was not writing the *Turneid,* but would he have been happier doing so?

The violent nature of Turnus, at once neurotic and attractive, has about it the aura of a Latin Hotspur, though Turnus lacks Hotspur's antic wit. But then Hotspur exists in a cosmos ultimately centered, not upon Bolingbroke the usurper and Prince Hal, but upon Falstaff, legitimate monarch of wit. Virgil is not exactly a humorous writer, and I suspect that, if he *was* in love with any of his own characters in the poem, it was with Turnus, rather than Dido, let alone Aeneas. The dreadful death of Turnus, which causes the poem to break off, in some sense is also the death of Virgil, or at least of Virgil's poetry:

> The man brought down, brought low, lifted his eyes
> And held his right hand out to make his plea:
>
> "Clearly I have earned this, and I ask no quarter.
> Make the most of your good fortune here.
> If you can feel a father's grief—and you, too,
> Had such a father in Anchises—then
> Let me bespeak your mercy for old age
> In Daunus, and return me, or my body,
> Stripped, if you will, of life, to my own kin.
> You have defeated me. The Ausonians
> Have seen me in defeat, spreading my hands.
> Lavinia is your bride. But go no further
> Out of hatred."
>
> Fierce under arms, Aeneas
> Looked to and fro, and towered, and stayed his hand
> Upon the sword-hilt. Moment by moment now
> What Turnus said began to bring him round
> From indecision. Then to his glance appeared
> The accurst swordbelt surmounting Turnus' shoulder,

> Shining with its familiar studs—the strap
> Young Pallas wore when Turnus wounded him
> And left him dead upon the field; now Turnus
> Bore that enemy token on his shoulder—
> Enemy still. For when the sight came home to him,
> Aeneas raged at the relic of his anguish
> Worn by this man as trophy. Blazing up
> And terrible in his anger, he called out:
>
> "You in your plunder, torn from one of mine,
> Shall I be robbed of you? This wound will come
> From Pallas: Pallas makes this offering
> And from your criminal blood exacts his due."
>
> He sank his blade in fury in Turnus' chest.
> Then all the body slackened in death's chill,
> And with a groan for that indignity
> His spirit fled into the gloom below.
>   (12.930–52, Fitzgerald translation)

The death of Turnus indeed is a terrible indignity, heroic neither for him nor for Aeneas. Turnus is truly slaughtered by Jove, who has been able to impose his will upon Juno, and then takes on something of her spirit when she yields. The Dira, manifesting as a gruesome carrion bird, sickens poor Turnus, numbing his giant force until he does not know himself. In a waking nightmare, unable to speak, standing defenseless, Turnus becomes merely an object into which Aeneas hurls a spear. Aeneas furiously stabbing to death a man already ruined by the Dira is hardly an Achilles or a Roland, and it is very good that the poem abruptly ends there. Could we forgive an Aeneas who exulted in such a triumph? Why does Virgil end his poem with so gratuitous a slaughter? Can he have intended to give us a Jupiter so contaminated by Juno? Such a Jupiter is more like a Gnostic Archon than in any way an Epicurean vision of the divine.

All we can be certain of is that Virgil deliberately wounds himself even as he wounds us. All of book 12 is an effective horror, an epiphany of lacerations and self-destroyings. I do not pretend to understand the scene in which Jupiter and Juno are reconciled to one another, and she agrees to give up her vendetta against the Trojans. Perhaps Virgil did not understand it either. If he was a convinced Epicurean, then he must have turned against his own rationality in his final vision of Jove, who is certainly not indifferent but positively malevolent, and pragmatically as sadistic as Juno. A passionately intense Valentinian Gnostic could have ended on no darker vision of the demonic, masquerading as the fury of God.

Against book 12, every reader rightly sets the poignance of book 6, and yet book 6 does not culminate the poem. It is well to remember that book 5 ends with the elegiac words of Aeneas to the memory of the lost helmsman, Palinurus:

> For counting
> Overmuch on a calm world, Palinurus,
> You must lie naked on some unknown shore.

Book 6 concludes with the passage of Aeneas and the Sibyl out of the world below by the Ivory Gate, and yet book 7 is Juno's book, and Allecto's, "with her lust for war, / For angers, ambushes, and crippling crimes." W. R. Johnson finds the poem's center, for him, in book 12, lines 665–69, where Turnus makes a great recovery:

> Stunned and confused
> By one and another image of disaster,
> Turnus held stock-still with a silent stare.
> In that one heart great shame boiled up, and madness
> Mixed with grief, and love goaded by fury,
> Courage inwardly known. When by and by
> The darkness shadowing him broke and light
> Came to his mind again, wildly he turned
> His burning eyes townward and from his car
> Gazed at the city.

That is magnificent, but each reader of the *Aeneid* chooses his or her own center. Mine is book 6, lines 303–14, always admired by readers through the generations:

> Here a whole crowd came streaming to the banks,
> Mothers and men, the forms of life all spent
> Of heroes great in valor, boys and girls
> Unmarried, and young sons laid on the pyre
> Before their parents' eyes—as many souls
> As leaves that yield their hold on boughs and fall
> Through forests in the early frost of autumn,

> Or as migrating birds from the open sea
> That darken heaven when the cold season comes
> And drives them overseas to sunlit lands.
> There all stood begging to be first across
> And reached out longing hands to the far shore.

Homer's fiction of the leaves as the human generations is transumed here with an inventiveness that has inspired poets from Dante to Spenser, Milton and Shelley, and on to Whitman and Wallace Stevens. What is, to me, peculiarly Virgilian and surpassingly beautiful is the movement from the tropes of the autumnal leaves and the migrating birds to the terrible pathos of the "pauper souls, the souls of the unburied," who must flutter and roam the wrong side of the black waters for a century. To stretch out one's longing hands to the farther shore, when that shore is oblivion, is a purely Virgilian figure, not Homeric, and has about it the uniquely Virgilian plangency. The *Aeneid* is a poem that attempts to compel itself to the grandeur of Augustan vistas, but its genius has little to do with Augustus, and at last little to do even with Aeneas. Of all the greater Western poems, it reaches out most longingly to the farther shore.

Aeneas

Viktor Pöschl

The angry crescendo of the tempest directs our attention to Aeneas with that sudden jolt found by Richard Heinze to be a favorite artistic device of Virgil: "*Extemplo Aeneae solvuntur frigore membra*" (1.92). He "enters with almost a fainting fit" (Saint-Beuve) and cries out in mortal fear:

> How fortunate were you, thrice fortunate and more, whose luck it was to die under the high walls of Troy before your parents' eyes! Ah, Diomede, most valiant of Greeks, why did your arm not strike me down and give my spirit freedom in death on the battlefields of Ilium, where lie the mighty Sarpedon, and Hector the manslayer, pierced by Achilles' lance, and where Simois rolls down submerged beneath his stream those countless shields and helms and all those valiant dead!

> O terque quaterque beati,
> Quis ante ora patrum Troiae sub moenibus altis
> Contigit oppetere! O Danaum fortissime gentis
> Tydide! Mene Iliacis occumbere campis
> Non potuisse tuaque animam hanc effundere dextra,
> Saevus ubi Aeacidae telo iacet Hector, ubi ingens
> Sarpedon, ubi tot Simois correpta sub undis
> Scuta virum galeasque et fortia corpora volvit?
>
> (1.94)

From *The Art of Vergil: Image and Symbol in the Aeneid.* © 1962 by the University of Michigan. University of Michigan Press, 1962.

This is a transformation of Odysseus's words (*Odyssey* 5.306): "Three times happy are the Danaans and four times who fell on the broad plains of Troy, in loyalty to the house of Atreus. If only I had died and met my destiny on the day when so many Trojans hurled their bronze spears against me over the dead son of Peleus. At least I would have been buried with all honor and the Achaeans would spread my name far and wide. But as it is I seem fated to die a sad death." But is it really no more than a quotation from Homer?

Odysseus grieves because he must forego glory and burial honors; he does not mention love. Aeneas's wish to have died "*ante ora patrum*" expresses not only longing for glory but also for love and warmth of home. The thought that the presence of loved ones blunts the sting of death, is a common motif in the *Aeneid*. Thus, Dido's death agony is eased by her sister's presence and by the gesture of release with which Juno sends Iris to shorten her suffering. The dying Camilla is assisted by her fellow-in-arms, Acca, before Diana carries her off. We hear of Aeneas's compassion for Palinurus and of Nisus sacrificing himself for Euryalus. Likewise, the battle death of Pallas and Lausus is relieved through Aeneas's mourning. Turnus and Mezentius die alone but with thoughts of those they love. Even the dead of Actium and the doomed Cleopatra are lovingly received by the god of the river Nile (8.711). That is the kind of death for which Aeneas has wished. Moreover, while Odysseus remembers only his own peril before Troy, Aeneas mentions the end of the great Trojan heroes, Hector and Sarpedon, and all the corpses which Simois turns over and over. Thus his ties with the dead comrades of his old home are clearly seen.

He appears as a man of memory and of inner vision. In the extremity of death and suffering the grief burning in his heart breaks out. His speech not only expresses his mortal fear, but also serves to express his character. It allows one a glimpse of his heart and of a basic motif of the poem. This is Virgil's own experience of what it means to be exiled from home, an experience that he had already expressed so movingly in the first *Eclogue*. The sorrowfully pathetic image which climaxes and ends his speech (Homer has no such climax), although inspired by Homer (*Iliad* 21.301), fits the storm at sea as perfectly as if invented especially for it. Shortly afterward the sad destructiveness of the storm is described with a similar image:

Arma virum tabulaeque at Troia gaza per undas

(1.119)

This is an echo of the *"correpta sub undis scuta virum."* And in it the struggle for a homogeneity of imagery and unity of key is clearly visible. The monologue of despair surpasses Homer both in form and content of feeling. By means of its inner correlation to the tempest imagery, it has become more ingenious and somehow deeper and more gentle, but less "natural" than its simple-ending Odyssean counterpart. "I, however, was destined to die a sad death." This loss of natural simplicity is the price paid for perfection of the classical form. The richer, more significant content and riper artistry could not be reconciled with Homer's simple strength.

The sorrowful memory of Troy, emphasized in Aeneas's first words, is a recurring leitmotif in the first third of the *Aeneid*. It recurs in the hero's speech to Venus (1.372): *"O dea si prima repetens ab origine pergam"*) and in his concentration on the Trojan War reliefs in Juno's temple in Carthage; it expands as the great narrative of the city's fall (2), flares up in the meetings with Polydorus, Helenus, and Andromache (3), and reappears in the scene with Dido when Aeneas speaks once more of his longing for Troy (4.430). Aeneas's close relationship to Hector, his predecessor as the Trojan leader, is also repeatedly revealed in these books, first in the description of the relief in which the particular importance of Hector's fate is emphasized in being set apart; again when Hector approaches the dreaming Aeneas in a decisive moment during Troy's last night (2.270ff.); then in the pathetic image of Andromache mourning over Hector's ashes (3.302ff.). Hector's personality is later conjured up in Aeneas's legacy to Ascanius, just before the decisive duel with Turnus:

> But when in due time your own age ripens to maturity, it will be for you to see to it that you do not forget, but recall in your thought the examples set you by your kindred. Your father is Aeneas and your uncle was Hector. Let that be your inspiration.

> Tu facito mox cum matura adoleverit aetas
> Sis memor et te animo repetentem exempla tuorum
> Et pater Aeneas et avunculus excitet Hector.
>
> (12.438)

Troy has gone, but Aeneas preserves its image and its heroes' glory, just as he saves its gods. His strength for founding a new Troy springs from a loving memory. Aeneas is the symbol of the mood existing between collapse and salvation, the chaos of civil war and the advent of Augustan peace.

The Trojan "Iliad" in the first third of the *Aeneid,* inserted in the Carthaginian events as reminiscent narrative and an "unspeakable," heavy burden upon the hero's soul, is counterpart to the Italian "Iliad" in the last third. This balanced way in which the Greco-Trojan past and the Roman future are incorporated into the poem is another example of the classical feeling for symmetry: the correlated parts are equated in form as well as content. The form is expression of organized thought.

The middle third contains, as it were, the hero's emancipation from the burden of the past. We are told how he leaves the *"animos nil magnae laudis egentis"* in Sicily under the rule of Acestes and founds a second Ilium for them (5). Then, after a final irresolution (5.700ff.) he turns decisively to his new task. The revelation granted him in the underworld completely fills him with the consciousness of his new mission. The thought of Troy, which has occupied his heart so far, is replaced. Memory becomes hope; retrospective longing for Troy gives way to a visionary longing for Rome. He turns from his ancestors to his descendants. The proem rising from *"Troiae ab oris"* in the first verse to *"altae moenia Romae"* in the last verse has clearly emphasized the beginning and the end of the way. *Rome* is the last word of the poem because it is the inner goal of the epic and the main theme of the poem. Even the arrangement of words points out what is important. The "historical" attitude of Aeneas expresses the moral change in Virgil's world and its difference from that of Homer's. Unlike Homer's heroes, the figure of Aeneas simultaneously comprises past, present, and future. Even in mortal extremity the past is with him: his actions spring from memory and hope. He is under the responsibility of history: *"Attollitque umero famamque et fata nepotum."* We might add: *"atque maiorum."* In the *Aeneid,* we see for the first time the tragedy of man suffering from historical fate. The hero is never allowed to belong completely to the moment. If and when, as in Carthage, he seems to be caught up in the moment, a god reminds him of his duty.

In the Homeric man the sensual present is supreme. The past may appear as memory and paradigm, the future as a fleeting glimpse, and sometimes—as in Homer's most tragic figure, Achilles—the knowledge of tragic destiny overwhelms the present. Sometimes, as in Zeus's speech to Achilles' horses, words expressing the poet's awareness of human tragedy are put into a god's mouth. But even though Homer's heroes feel sorrow as keenly as Aeneas does, they appear to forget it more easily.

Aeneas's sorrow is never forgotten; it is always ready to break forth from the bottom of his heart. Homeric heroes are not so constantly overshadowed by their melancholies. It is true that the Odyssean figures are subject to some secret longing which brings the soul to light, for when the soul's light falls on the senses, the present fades. In the *Odyssey* we see a shift in emphasis on the importance of the moment and that of the soul. Still, the soul is *in absentia* for long periods. In contrast to the Aeneas of the book of wanderings, Homer's Odysseus, in relating his adventures, is completely enmeshed by current events, and his longing, when it emerges, is confined to the small area of his individual life. It is easy to imagine what Virgil would have done with the subject matter of the *Odyssey*—how he would have enhanced the inner life of the soul and the impact of history and decreased the importance of the sensual present.

Past and future in Homer never extend to such psychological depths and historical distances. The scope of the Greek epic falls short of the scope of the Roman *Aeneid*. It was the Roman poet, Virgil, who discovered the grievous burden of history and its vital meaning. He was the first to perceive deeply the cost of historical greatness; Jacob Burckhardt much later restated the same insight. Aeneas's attitude comes from a superior historical consciousness, developed by the Romans beyond that of the Greeks, and from the characteristic Roman feeling for time insofar as the present was evaluated as only a part of temporal totality and was always connected with historical past and future. In a deeper sense, past and future are always present inasmuch as they give weight and value to the moment.

Moreover, Aeneas's attitude testifies to the Roman sense of duty which is in sharp contrast to the Greek sense of existence, for whatever the Homeric heroes do, they do in fulfillment of their nature rather than their duty. Aeneas, however, is a hero of duty, while Dido is a tragic heroine because she suffers from the guilty consciousness of her violated duty as does Turnus from the god-inflicted delusion on his. The *Aeneid* would not be the ideal expression of *res Romana* that it is, if the fulfillment of duty were not fundamental to its hero. The peculiar content of the modern concept of duty is a consequence of Roman morality. The early structures of family and state rest upon this concept and wherever it appears later, as in the Christian ethics of both Kant and Schiller, the influence of Roman thought is effective. This is one of the reasons Schiller felt so deeply attracted to Virgil.

To the hero, Aeneas, the memory of Troy and the hope for Rome are holy obligations, and in their fulfillment he displays *pietas* which is nothing else but doing his duty to gods, country, ancestors, and descendants. "Duty" here, however, is not a response to the dictates of reason, but a response to love, and is without the harsh associations evoked by the word.

The "Homeric quotation" of Aeneas's first words proves to be a farther-reaching transformation of its model than is immediately evident. The outer and inner structure of the *Aeneid* transforms the simple thought of the *Odyssey* into an integral part of itself. After these words, the storm grows more intense and the description of its ravages rises in two climactic peaks, and in comparison with the Homeric storms in the fifth and twelfth books of the *Odyssey,* the accent shifts decidedly. First there is the sinking of the Lycian ship bearing "faithful Orontes"—an epithet which in itself shows the poet's compassion and some measure of the tragedy of Aeneas. In sharp contrast is the Homeric counterpart where Odysseus, himself and not the poet, describes the death of the pilot, his skull smashed by the mast so that he plunges into the sea "like a diver." He tells of the sad fate of his companions "dancing" like seagulls on the waves. He reports the death of his fellows with vivid accuracy but without visible emotional involvement. Even in a speech Homer is objective in viewpoint. Even in narrative Virgil remains subjective. Another climax comes in the words "*Troiae gaza per undas,*" which signify part of the tragedy within Aeneas—the loss of his keepsakes from Troy. They are important, too, in concluding the description proper of the tempest.

Here, then, are an inner and an outer climax: Aeneas's mortal fear increases and is yet surpassed by the feelings aroused in him at the loss of Orontes and the *gaza Troiae*. Here, too, the final climax is the tragedy of Troy.

If Aeneas's first words show his *pietas* above all, his comforting address to his companions after the rescue (198ff.) reveals still another fundamental feature of his character—his *magnitudo animi*.

> We have forced our way through adventures of every kind, risking all again; but the way is the way to Latium, where Destiny offers us rest and a home, and where imperial Troy may have the right to live again. Hold hard, therefore. Preserve yourselves for better days.

> Per varios casus, per tot discrimina rerum
> Tendimus in Latium, sedes ubi fata quietas

> Ostendunt: illic fas regna resurgere Troiae.
> Durate et vosmet rebus servate secundis.
>
> (1.204)

Virgil intensifies the impression of Aeneas's *magnitudo animi* by showing it against the backdrop of his sorrow and grief:

> He was sick at heart, for the cares which he bore were heavy indeed. Yet he concealed his sorrow deep within him, and his face looked confident and cheerful.
>
> > Curisque ingentibus aeger
> > Spem voltu simulat, premit altum corde dolorem.
> >
> > (1.208)

This speech is considerably different from Odysseus's words to his comrades, which it recalls (12.208ff.). Homer's Odysseus is a brave man, who in a perilous situation (between Scylla and Charybdis) gives intelligent and prudent orders. On the other hand, Virgil's Aeneas is a great soul, pressing toward a magnificent goal. Like the first, the second speech culminates in the thought of Troy and its renascent empire to come. In this we see that Virgil differs from Homer in the monumentalization and transformation of something of specific importance into something of general importance; he removed epic reality from a too intimate contact with objective detail to weave the transparency of a larger scene.

Aeneas's first speeches reveal his basic character; they are inwardly and outwardly integral to the whole work because the poet concentrates completely on the essential and significant from the very beginning. However, this tendency to reveal basic traits of character and destiny upon the first appearance of an individual is also occasionally noticeable in Homer's much more loosely composed epic. It is seen, for example, in the sixth book of the *Iliad,* when Hector, failing to find Andromache at home, hears that she is neither with her family nor in the temple of Athena; on learning that the Trojans are being defeated and that the Achaeans' power is growing stronger, she has gone to the great tower of Ilium. In her gesture of madly rushing to the wall, with the nurse carrying the child, her gentle and passionate soul is given expression. The poet need say nothing of her love, for the gesture expresses it better than words could. This is our introduction to Andromache! The scene simultaneously intimates Hector's destiny, for on a deeper level of understanding, Andromache's concern is revealed as tragic premonition.

The connection is not so obvious with the other characters in the

Iliad, though their first appearance is characteristic. The manner in which Agamemnon screams at Chryses points up his violent and selfish nature, and Thetis instantly shows herself as a loving mother when in response to Achilles' prayer she rises like mist from the sea to caress her son. In his censure of Paris, Hector proves himself an unyielding defender of his people's honor and their true leader. In this expression of long-suppressed resentment he uncovers his passionate nature. But the connection with the development of the story is not so definite. The strict integration of detail with the whole, of words and gestures with character, of character with destiny, of destiny with the structure of the plot—all essentials in the *Aeneid*—are less well developed in the *Iliad*. So there is less immediacy in the establishment of the principle of classical composition, according to which each part receives its true importance only through its relation to the whole. The introduction of a course of events is more leisurely, so there is more opportunity for involvement with each character.

The situation in the *Odyssey* is somewhat different, and this fact must not be ignored in a criticism of the two epics. There, the initial entrance of the main figures is fashioned with great care and harmonious variation around one idea—the longing for the hero's return and the grief over his absence. In an unforgettable picture, Odysseus appears looking tearfully out on the rushing sea. Unable to bear her grief, Penelope descends from her suite to make the minstrel stop singing of the Achaeans' return. At the approach of Athena in the guise of Mentor, Telemachos looks at the gate because in his mind's eye he sees his father coming to chase away the plague of suitors. Eumaios, after driving off the dogs which threaten the stranger, begins immediately to speak of his grief for his absent master. Each one is occupied by a single great feeling of longing which is the main content of his life.

Let us now return to the trials of Aeneas. The basic forces in Aeneas's soul, respect for duty, firmness of resolution, and human feeling appear in the decisive moment of the Dido crisis. The climax of the fourth book of the *Aeneid* comes after Queen Dido's plea to Aeneas to change his cruel decision to leave her:

> He, remembering Jupiter's warning, held his eyes steady, and strained to master the agony within him.

> Ille Iovis monitis immota tenebat
> Lumina et obnixus curam sub corde premebat.
>
> (4.331)

The expression *"obnixus curam,"* etc., is very similar to *"premit altum corde dolorem"* (1.209), except that more emphasis is given to the mag-nitude of effort. However, it is not so much the passion of his love that moves Aeneas, as is assumed by modern interpretation, for Virgil has treated this feeling with the greatest reserve. Rather, he is moved by compassion for Dido's grief. And this compassion, heightened by love, is a manifestation of *humanitas,* which, according to the command of the gods, is suppressed. Aeneas's painful resignation is not a renunciation of love, then, but a response to the gods' prohibition. He is not permitted to relieve the grieving queen, but is forced by his religious duty to gods and progeny to neglect his human duty to Dido. He suffers more because of the sorrow for others than because of his own misfortune. His concern to protect those near to him from grief and pain never slackens. This protective feeling finds its most beautiful expression in the *Iliupersis:*

> And now, though up till then I had remained quite unaffected
> by any weapons or even the sight of Greeks charging towards
> me, I myself was now ready to be frightened at a breath of
> wind and started at the slightest sound, so nervous was I, and
> so fearful alike for the load on my back and the companion
> at my side.

> > Et me quem dudum non ulla iniecta movebant
> > Tela neque adverso glomerati ex agmine Grai,
> > Nunc omnes terrent aurae, sonus excitat omnis
> > Suspensum et pariter comitique onerique timentem.
> > > (2.726)

When Dido, upon being refused, hurls her curse at the hero and is carried into the marble chamber by her maids, the same sorrowful determination is found in heightened form:

> Meanwhile Aeneas the True longed to allay her grief and dispel
> her sufferings with kind words. Yet he remained obedient to
> the divine command, and with many a sigh, for he was
> shaken to the depths by the strength of his love, returned to
> his ships.

> > At pius Aeneas, quamquam lenire dolentem
> > Solando cupit et dictis avertere curas,
> > Multa gemens magnoque animum labefactus amore,
> > Iussa tamen divom exsequitur.
> > > (4.393)

Even more intensified, the motif returns for the third time following Anna's final attempt to change the departing hero's mind. Here, Aeneas's inner struggle is given mighty expression in the oak simile. This simile, symbol of Aeneas's heroic manner, is closely related to that inner strength so prized by the Stoics. In this connection, it is interesting to note that Seneca compares the wise man to a storm-buffeted tree—perhaps with the *Aeneid* in mind:

> Like a strong oak-tree toughened by the years when northern winds from the Alps vie together to tear it from the soil, with their blasts striking on it now this side and now that; creaking, the trunk shakes, and leaves from on high strew the ground; yet still the tree grips among the rocks below, for its roots stretch as far down towards the abyss as its crest reaches up to the airs of heaven. Like that tree, the hero was battered this side and that by their insistent pleas, and deeply his brave heart grieved, but without effect.

> Ac velut annoso validam cum robore quercum
> Alpini Boreae nunc hinc nunc flatibus illinc
> Eruere inter se certant, it stridor et altae
> Consternunt terram concusso stipite frondes,
> Ipsa haeret scopulis et quantum vertice ad auras
> Aetherias tantum radice in Tartara tendit:
> Haud secus adsiduis hinc atque hinc vocibus heros
> Tunditur et magno persentit pectore curas,
> Mens immota manet, lacrimae volvuntur inanes.
>   (4.441)

The *lacrimae inanes* are the tears which Aeneas sheds in vain; they have no effect on his unshakable resolution. In contrast to all modern commentators, Augustine and Servius have interpreted this passage correctly. To make these the tears of Anna or Dido would be to weaken the impact considerably, for the emphasis is not so much on the contest between Aeneas and Anna as on the hero's divided heart and his painful resignation. The meaning of this simile, then, can be understood only as an image of this inner struggle or as an expression of the bitter contest between hard and fast resolution and his human heart. Once the overpowering nature of this battle is understood, no other interpretation is acceptable. The bold inner antithesis is much to be preferred to the lame outer one. The oak suffers, too, as is indicated by its groaning and the image *"altae consternunt terram concusso stipite frondes."* As Servius has observed (*"frondes sicut lacrimae Aeneae"*), there is a distinct inner relation between Aeneas's tears and the leaves shed by the tree, for there are fewer superfluous features in Virgil's similes than in Homer's. Here, the essence of the simile is "suffering." The oak is similar to the fallen mountain ash which symbolizes the fall of Troy in the *Iliupersis*. There too the simile, quite un-Homerically, does not illustrate an event, but expounds a destiny. The suffering of the tree—its "tragedy"—is the main thing:

> Like an ancient rowan tree high up among the mountains, which, hacked with stroke after stroke of iron axes by farmers vying all round to dislodge it, begins to tremble and continues threatening while the crest shakes and the high boughs sway, till gradually vanquished it gives a final groan, and at last overcome by the wounds and wrenched from its place it trails havoc down the mountain-side.

> > Ac veluti summis antiquam in montibus ornum
> > Cum ferro accisam crebrisque bipennibus instant
> > Eruere agricolae certatim; illa usque minatur
> > Et tremefacta comam concusso vertice nutat,
> > Volneribus donec paulatim evicta supremum
> > Congemuit traxitque iugis avolsa ruinam.
> > > (2.626)

Hercules, too, conquers his grief at the death of Pallas and yet sheds *lacrimas inanes*:

> Hercules heard the young man's prayer. Deep in his heart he repressed a heavy sigh; and his tears streamed helplessly.

> > Audiit Alcides iuvenem magnumque sub imo
> > Corde premit gemitum lacrimasque effundit inanes.
> > > (10.464)

The inner relation of these passages is another proof that it is Aeneas who weeps—not Anna. Thus, the allegory of his sublime grandeur that concludes an important section of the fourth book ends with an antithesis which once more points out the strength of his resolution and the sorrow in his heart. It is worthwhile noting that this scene concludes with tears. The hero's humanity is stressed at a moment when he could easily seem cruel. On the whole, the contrast between Aeneas's coolness and Dido's ardor is the original tragic contrast between man and woman as it has been shaped in modern art, by say, Heine and Boécklin. The relation of the Aeneas-Dido antithesis to that between Jupiter and Juno has been mentioned [elsewhere].

Here, a simile signifies the sorrowful resolution of the hero; at the beginning of the fifth book a symbolic gesture does the same thing:

> Aeneas and his fleet were now far out to sea. He set course resolutely and ploughed through waves ruffled to black by a northerly wind. As he sailed he looked back to walled Carthage, now aglow with tragic Dido's flames.

> Interea medium Aeneas iam classe tenebat
> Certus iter fluctusque atros aquilone secabat
> Moenia respiciens, quae iam infelicis Elissae
> Conlucent flammis.
>
> (5.1)

Steadfastly, he follows his course in spite of storm and the memory of Dido (clearly reflected in the words *"moenia respiciens"*). He does so in spite of the glow of the funeral pyre the flames of which awaken dark premonitions in the hearts of the Trojans. Servius's explanation: *"certus: indubitabiliter pergens, id est itineris sui certus,"* approved by Heyne and rejected by Wagner, is basically correct. Although *certus* refers immediately to the straight course of the fleet, the straight course, itself, symbolizes the hero's firm determination. . . .

Within [this image], however, is the great idea that Aeneas's journey and the whole poem are a simile of the life of man. Even in antiquity the *Odyssey* was so interpreted. Of course, there is no question of applying the simplified form of allegorical-philosophical interpretation exemplified, say, by the well-known epistle of Horace (1.2), but there can be no doubt that Virgil was well acquainted with it and that the *Aeneid* is a simile in this sense, too.

Aeneas's firmness in the midst of trouble and confusion is shown in other symbolic gestures. Recall the words following the death of Palinurus at the end of the fifth book:

> Therefore he steered her himself through the midnight waves with many a sigh, for he was deeply shocked by the disaster to his friend.

> Ipse ratem nocturnis rexit in undis,
> Multa gemens casuque animum concussus amici.
>
> (5.868)

Here, again, the symbolic meaning of the sea voyage appears. There is sublime simplicity and transparent beauty in image and expression. Another example is the beginning of the eleventh book, which in composition of the whole corresponds to the beginning of the fifth:

> The morrow's rising dawn had emerged from the ocean. Aeneas, deeply burdened as he was by thoughts of death, would naturally have preferred to devote his time to giving his comrades burial. But instead at first light from the east he started to fulfill his vows to the gods in return for his victory.

> Oceanum interea surgens Aurora reliquit,
> Aeneas, quamquam et sociis dare tempus humandis
> Praecipitant curae turbataque funere mens est,
> Vota deum primo victor solvebat Eoo.
>
> (11.1)

Compare the pathetically determined and restrained gesture *"nec plura effatus"* with which he turns back from the corpse of Pallas to the camp:

> After the whole procession had gone on far ahead, Aeneas halted, and with a heavy sigh spoke again: "We are called hence to other tears by this same grim destiny of war. Pallas, great hero, I bid you forever hail, and forever farewell." Saying no more he moved off towards his own high defence-works and walked back into his camp.

> Postquam omnis longe comitum praecesserat ordo,
> Substitit Aeneas gemituque haec edidit alto:
> Nos alias hinc ad lacrimas eadem horrida belli
> Fata vocant. Salve aeternum mihi, maxume Palla,
> Aeternumque vale. Nec plura effatus ad altos
> Tendebat muros gressumque in castra ferebat.
>
> (11.94)

Here one senses how deeply the poet is affected by the bitterness of war; beneath Aeneas's grief for Pallas flashes a greater tragedy of which his friend's death is only one instance symbolizing the long procession of dead to follow him—the "other tears." In such moments Aeneas is the personification of the feeling of tragedy which is basic to the poem. It is true that all figures created by the poet represent dialectical possibilities of his own soul, but Aeneas represents the innermost core. Virgil's "psychography" may be drawn from Aeneas's personality. The sensitivity to tragedy which characterizes the hero is the same sensitivity with which the poet himself looks at the world and life. It is the compassionate eye with which the Virgilian gods regard the fighting:

> In Jupiter's palace the gods pitied the pointless fury of both sides, sad that men doomed in any case to die, should suffer ordeals so terrible.

> > Di Iovis in tectis iram miserantur inanem
> > Amborum et tantos mortalibus esse labores.
> > > (10.758ff.)

Theirs is the astonished sorrow to which Virgil gives voice at the beginning: "*Tantaene animis caelestibus irae?*" It breaks forth again and again from Aeneas—and from him alone. We hear it in the woeful exclamation: "*Heu quantae miseris caedes Laurentibus instant?*" (8.537). Or, most nearly related in content to the first question, in the hero's words to the Latins when they ask for a truce to bury their dead:

> Ah, Latins, how unjustly and unhappily you have been involved in this terrible war which leads you to shrink from friendship with us!

> > Quaenam vos tanto fortuna indigna, Latini,
> > Implicuit bello, qui nos fugiatis amicos.
> > > (11.108)

It finds its highest form in Aeneas's journey through the underworld, since this journey is a symbol of Virgil's experience of the tragedy of life. The guilt, atonement, and suffering he encounters there awaken in him tragically compassionate sorrow—the same enormous sympathy characteristic of his actions and sufferings elsewhere and explicitly stated in the case of Dido:

> Aeneas was shocked by her unjust fate; and as she went long gazed after her with tearful eyes and pity for her in his heart.

Nec minus Aeneas *casu concussus iniquo*
Prosequitur lacrimis longe et *miseratur* euntem.
(6.475).

This compassion is the most pathetic when he sees the souls along the river Lethe "drink the waters which abolish care and give enduring release from memory" in order to return to the world:

Oh, Father, am I therefore to believe that of those souls some go, soaring hence, up to the world beneath our sky and return once more into dreary matter? Why should the poor souls so perversely desire the light of our day?

O pater, anne aliquas ad caelum hinc ire putandum est
Sublimis animas iterumque ad tarda reverti
Corpora? Quae lucis miseris tam dira cupido?

(6.719)

It seems rather like a palinode on Achilles' lament in the *Odyssey*. Achilles would prefer being a hired hand of the poorest man to being a king in the shadowy world of the dead. This is the same Platonism as that of Cicero in the *Somnium Scipionis*. In both cases the soul acquainted with grief finds comfort in expressing its sorrow. Why these passages spoke so eloquently to the hearts of coming generations, filled as they were with an ever-growing longing for redemption, is plain.

Aeneas, measuring his own fate against the better fortune of others, similarly perceived its tragic quality:

How fortunate were you, thrice fortunate and more, whose luck it was to die under the high walls of Troy before your parents' eyes!

O terque quaterque beati
Quis ante ora patrum Troiae sub moenibus altis
Contigit oppetere.

(1.94)

Aeneas looked up at the buildings. "Ah, fortunate people," he exclaimed, "for your city-walls are already rising!"

O fortunati, quorum iam moenia surgunt,
Aeneas ait et fastigia suspicit urbis.

(1.437)

Live, and prosper, for all your adventures are past. We are
called ever onward from destiny to destiny. For you, your rest
is won. You have no expanse of sea to plough, no land of
Italy, seeming always to recede before you, as your quest.

> Vivite felices, quibus est fortuna peracta
> Iam sua, nos alia ex aliis in fata vocamur.
> Vobis parta quies, nullum maris aequor arandum
> Arva neque Ausoniae semper cedentia retro
> Quaerenda.
>
> (3.493ff.)

"From me, my son," he said, "you may learn what is valour
and what is strenuous toil; as for what good fortune is, others
must teach you that."

> Disce, puer, virtutem ex me verumque laborem,
> Fortunam ex aliis.
>
> (12.435)

No matter how often sorrow overwhelms his sensitive heart, he shows
heroism by passing through it, by "leading his life through all extrem-
ities" (3.315: "*vivo equidem vitamque extrema per omnia duco*"), mastering
inner torment (*premit altum corde dolorem*), and yielding to destiny in noble
resignation. Thus, he illustrates what Schopenhauer expected of poetry:
the power to save us from sentimentality and to raise us to resignation.
The grief that Aeneas bears and conquers is, I repeat, less sorrow for
his own lost or denied happiness than sympathy and compassion for
others who must suffer bitterly for the sake of the command laid on him
by destiny. Homer's heroes suffer through "love of self" in the high
Aristotelian sense. And Virgil's other protagonists, Dido and Turnus,
suffer in a similar way; but Aeneas suffers for the sake of others. A new
humanity announcing the Christian philosophy bursts forth in him. He
prefigures the Christian hero, whose heart remains gentle through strug-
gle and sorrow and beats in secret sympathy with all suffering creatures.

Virgil also reshaped the idea of duty, which, always a primary
element of Roman ethics, is a decisive factor in Aeneas's behavior. In
infusing it with deep humanity, he brought it close to the Christian idea
of charity and solidarity. This is one of the main reasons why Virgil
became a mediator between the antique Roman world and medieval
Christianity.

It follows, therefore, from this line of thought that the "Stoic" interpretation of Aeneas, as proposed by Heinze, cannot be correct—at least not if the concept is accepted in its strict sense. The hero experiences sorrow, especially spiritual sorrow, to the utmost. It is always his moral goal to do what is necessary in spite of his great sensitivity and never to make himself insensitive. It is precisely because of this that he affects us as a tragic hero. It enhances the impression of his will power, for it is necessary that he have the heroic spiritual strength in order to conquer the sorrows of which he is acutely aware. Virgil widens the distance between the longing in Aeneas's sensitive heart and the harsh demands of destiny, while the Stoic doctrine, on the contrary, hardens and silences the heart with overpowering reason. Although it is true that Aeneas's is the noble sorrow of compassion, it must be remembered that the Stoa did not allow the wise man even this feeling.

Far from aspiring to ataraxia, Aeneas strives to deny sorrow's influence upon his actions rather than to obliterate it through reason. Here, the affinity to Christianity is unmistakable, for in the depth of his being he turns *toward* his sorrow rather than away from it. True, St. Augustine is right, as pointed out earlier, in claiming that the verse *"mens immota manet: lacrimae volvuntur inanes"* is an example of Ciceronian and Middle Stoic thought, according to which there is no difference between Peripatetic and Stoic attitudes toward suffering. But this applies only to the Middle Stoa of Panaitios which was bent on lessening the contrasts between the schools in favor of a middle way. It does not apply to the strict Stoa; the sorrow of Aeneas could not pass its censure. His "stoic" attitude toward the wound (12.398), his apparent insensibility in the face both of physical pain and the sympathy of his comrades (characteristically emphasized more) is the result of his indignation at the Latins' breach of contract, as is his impetuous rage to meet Turnus in battle. The violation of the truce changes him into an angry warrior, dead-set upon merciless destruction of his opponent to satisfy the demand of *"debellare superbos."* Outraged justice obliterates any other consideration. Here and only here, he is called "avidus pugnae" (12.430).

Seen in this way, Aeneas's attitude toward pain is by no means "stoic." Rather, perhaps, his perception of destiny as a school of suffering can be interpreted as "stoic." He opposes the wild prophecy of the Cumaean sybil concerning the bloody battles awaiting the Trojans, with the words:

> Maid, no aspect of tribulation which is new to me or unforeseen can rise before me, for I have traced my way through all that may happen in the anticipation of my inward thought.

> Non ulla laborum,
> O virgo, nova mi facies inopinave surgit;
> Omnia praecepi atque animo mecum ante peregi.
> (6.103)

The words and his serene attitude form a wonderful contrast with the furor of the priestess. Norden has noted the parallels in his commentary. Elsewhere, too, Aeneas's attitude toward fate may be considered as related to that of the Stoics, for example:

> Instead, my own valor, holy oracles from gods, my kinship between your father and mine, and your own renown throughout the world have all joined me to you and brought me here in willing obedience to my destiny.

> Sed mea me virtus et sancta oracula divom
> Cognatique patres, tua terris didita fama
> Coniunxere tibi et *fatis egere volentem*.
> (8.131)

But there is not always inner acquiescence to fate in Aeneas.

> Italiam non sponte sequor.
> (4.361)

> Invitus regina tuo de litore cessi,
> Sed me iussa deum . . . imperiis egere suis.
> (6.460)

When, after the burning of the ships, Aeneas, "*casu concussus iniquo*" (a recurring phrase no less characteristic of his justice than his humanity), is wavering again, the old Nautes reminds him of the claim of the Stoic attitude:

> Son of the Goddess, we should accept the lead which Destiny offers us, whether to go forward or not, and choose our way accordingly. Whatever is to befall, it is always our own power of endurance which must give us control over our fortune.

> Nate dea, quo fata trahunt retrahuntque sequamur;
> Quidquid erit, superanda omnis fortuna ferendo est.
> (5.709)

And in Aeneas's last words to Ascanius the poet restates, as it were, the hero's testament by foretelling the dark doom which will threaten him after Turnus's death:

> From me, my son, he said, you may learn what is valor and what is strenuous toil; as for what good fortune is, others must teach you that.

> Disce, puer, virtutem ex me verumque laborem,
> Fortunam ex aliis.
>
> (12.435)

There is no trace of the gladiatorial challenge and "*ostentatio*" toward fate, the most impressive form of which can perhaps be found in Seneca's *De Providentia*. That he should hate to have his son inherit his *fortuna*— his grievous destiny—shows not only his love for Ascanius, but also a sorrowful pity for his own and other people's sorrow which is anything but Stoic. And in spite of individual points of resemblance, Aeneas's attitude toward fate cannot be called "stoic" without reservations.

That poetic and philosophic perception of fate can never completely coincide was persuasively pointed out by Grillparzer in his essay on fate—and this should be remembered. These concepts are fundamentally different forms of the understanding of reality. It is true that the poetic world can partake of the philosophic world, but it can never be completely absorbed by it or identical with it. The poetic world obeys other laws. What Goethe wrote to Schiller apropos of his conversation with Schelling is of general significance: (In me) "philosophy destroys poetry." The ideal of a Stoic sage could never appear in a poem in its pure form without destroying its poetic character. For the rest, strict Stoicism cannot be expected of Virgil since it would contradict the spirit of the age. Cicero, the herald of the Augustan consciousness, had followed Panaitios in Hellenizing and humanizing the Stoa. The later Roman Stoa likewise did not adhere to strict doctrine. Seneca, himself, of whose attitude the above-mentioned *De Providentia* is by no means characteristic, is on the whole far removed from old Stoic rigidity and extremism. He is dedicated to a humane, liberal point of view which is continued later in the mild Stoicism of Marcus Aurelius.

The character of Aeneas is determined by an amalgamation of several traits: Homeric heroism, early Roman Stoic "*magnitudo animi*," and Virgilio-Augustan "*humanitas*" combined into a new whole. Should the "stoic" component prevail, the harmony of this vision of man would disappear. The proud sensitivity as well as the greatness of both Aeneas and Dido rests on the tension between *"magnitudo animi"* and *"human-itas."* Any interpretation that emphasizes either the stoic heroism in Aeneas's character or his sensitivity to the exclusion of the other, is false. It is also false to see him as too hard or too soft, too stoically Roman or too much like a modern Christian. And there is an analogous situation for Dido. In Virgil there is both the granite of ancient Roman grandeur and the delicate bloom of humanity opening upon a new dimension of the soul and destined to have a decisive influence on developing Christianity.

In this connection one more problem deserves discussion: the hero Aeneas's "character development." Heinze has attempted to state such a development. From the despair attending the tempest and the depression expressed in the monologue: *"O terque quaterque beati"* and the address *"O socii,"* Aeneas grows in steadfastness and stature. In the beginning, according to Heinze, he fails to personify the Stoic ideal, but finally reaches it in the course of his inner development. I do not believe that the modern concept of character development applies here. It is true that the stature of the hero grows with the situations according to the law of the intensification which governs the poem. This is true in the sense that the hero's character proves itself on an ever-enlarging level and that his inner strength increases with the gradual revelation of his mission. It is not true, however, in the sense of a progressive approximation to the ideal Stoic sage, nor in the sense of an inner development, the psychology of which would not have attracted the Homerizing poet. His character, or that which is the mark of his existence, remains unchanged; the conflict of heroic fulfillment of duty with human sensitivity that determines the shape of his existence pervades the whole poem. It is evident in the first scenes and can be followed to the last verses where he hesitates between killing and pardoning Turnus.

Moreover, the address must not be seen as expressing a lack of wisdom or incomplete self-discipline or faltering faith in God. On the contrary, the determination in these words is all the more admirable when we see that beneath them lies doubt and even despair. He is even here, as the sibyl will later ask him to be, *"audentior quam eius fortuna sinit."* Still, it is true that he passes through much suffering. Perhaps the formula *"Vivo equidem vitamque extrema per omnia duco"* best describes his condition. His potentiality for experiencing sorrow grows with the realization of the greatness of his task. The difference between the Aeneas of the last third of the poem and that of the first third lies not in his greater courage but in his greater experience and in his being more deeply pervaded by Roman attitudes. The sixth to eighth books contain the essential kernel of the poem in that the hero meets Rome physically and spiritually. In the sixth book he finds the Roman idea; in the seventh and eighth books he meets the Roman soil and landscape, the Roman cult and the λιτοδίαιτον of the Roman style of living. Moreover, these books contain religious and political-historical revelations which give a necessary importance and a significant frame to his actions. In the sixth book Aeneas is not only introduced to the tragic fate of this world and the solution and atonement to come in the world hereafter, but also to the order of this world and the course and meaning of Roman history. The eighth book also contains a lesson in that the straightforward simplicity of the old Roman morality is given to Aeneas as a model to be followed. In introducing the guest into his house, Evander formulates the "moral" of the book:

> Hercules himself in the hour of victory bowed his head to enter this door. This royal dwelling was not too small to contain even him. Guest of mine, be strong to scorn wealth and so mold yourself that you also may be fit for a God's converse. Be not exacting as you enter a poor home.

> haec, inquit, limina victor
> Alcides subiit, haec illum regia cepit.
> Aude, hospes, contemnere opes et te quoque dignum
> Finge deo, rebusque veni non asper egenis.
>
> (8.362)

In the eyes of his enemies, the Trojan king, Aeneas, was a rich Asiatic prince who had yielded to Punic luxury and was tainted with oriental effeminacy. Remember Jarbas's prayer in which Aeneas, the "Paris with a retinue of eunuchs and his perfumed hair," is oriental effeminacy personified; and the anger of Turnus (12.97) and the harsh words of Numanus that contrasted the old Italian *duritia* with the Phrygian *desidia* (9.603ff.). In Evander's house Aeneas is cleansed, as it were, of the odium of his Asiatic origin and imbued with Italo-Roman contempt for *luxuria*. In leaving the Oriental world and entering the Roman world, Aeneas becomes a Roman in his heart. This then is the deeper meaning of the eighth book as it concerns Aeneas's inner pilgrimage. And it follows convincingly that at the end of the book—in a prominent place, where the middle third of the poem ends—he should lift the shield of Vulcan whereon Roman history is shown as culminating in Augustus's victory and triumph: "Lifting the glory and destiny of the grandsons upon his shoulders." The vicarious character of his sufferings and actions could not be expressed more earnestly. At last he has acquired the necessary maturity to bear the destiny of Rome. Symbols of the Roman mission and scenes in which he personifies Roman majesty mark the places in the last books in which his appearance is most powerful.

Virgil's Style

Thomas Greene

The loss of Virgil to the modern world is an immeasurable cultural tragedy. For we have lost in him not only one of the greatest of world poets but also the master of European poetry. Ignorant of him, we are ignorant of aspects of other poets we think we know better. Virgil's earlier poetry was taught in Roman schools even before his death, and from then on, from the first century to the nineteenth, he was generally at the core of European education. More than the Bible (so little read in so many places at so many times), far more than Homer, Virgil has been *the* classic of Western civilization. This has been true partly because he is more fitly a poet of maturity than of youth, because his work continues to educate as the understanding ripens. Fully to know him, one must know him long. If he teaches the schoolboy style, to the man he imparts nobility.

The very word *nobility* is suspect in an age which has seen the decline of Virgil's influence. The word has overtones of snobbery and social privilege, and its moral associations suggest today an offensive pretentiousness, a shallow posturing, a cardboard dignity, qualities wholly un-Virgilian which he would have considered vulgar. Nobility in Virgil is concerned with authenticity, labor, and humility; it involves above all a spiritual generosity and an incapacity for triviality. Second-rate imitators of Virgil . . . have tried to achieve nobility by the artificial exclusion of commonplace things, but he himself wrote cheerfully about

From *The Descent from Heaven: A Study in Epic Continuity.* © 1963 by Thomas Greene. Yale University Press, 1963.

fertilizers. Our own century, reacting against that artificial exclusion, has embraced the commonplace and the trivial, so that a whole generation of poets has felt obliged to strew their work with the bric-a-brac of recent civilization. The same misplaced conscientiousness leads Day Lewis doggedly to measure out his clichés for each line of the *Aeneid*:

> To speak with brutal frankness
> And lay all my cards on the table—please take to heart
>   what I'm saying—
> I never had the right to promise my daughter.
>   [C. Day Lewis, *The Aeneid of Virgil* (London, 1952).]

The high style of the original Latin is earned by the high style of its author's feeling—style which cannot easily be imitated but to which one rises slowly, out of respect and emulation. In those rare places where the *Aeneid* courts the danger of flatulence, where the trumpets begin to sound a little too sonorously, Virgil's native magnanimity almost always saves him. Thus when, in the eighth book, Venus anticipates her gift of arms by a series of thunder crashes and a celestial vision of the gift, the potential emptiness of this grandiloquence is filled by the subsequent speech of Aeneas:

> "heu quantae miseris caedes Laurentibus instant!
> quas poenas mihi, Turne, dabis! quam multa sub undas
> scuta virum galeasque et fortia corpora volves,
> Thybri pater! poscant acies et foedera rumpant."

"Oh, piteous, that such fearful massacre hangs over the poor Laurentine people! Terrible, Turnus, is the penalty which you shall pay to me! And, Father Tiber, how many the valiant men, how many their shields and helms, which shall be swept rolling down beneath your waves! Now, let them break our compact! Now let them insist on battle!"

> [8.537–40; All the Latin quotations from Virgil in this chapter are taken from Virgil, *Opera,* ed. F. A. Hirtzel (Oxford, 1959). All the translations of Virgil are taken from *The Aeneid,* trans. W. F. Jackson Knight (Baltimore, Penguin Classics, 1962).]

Aeneas's joy at this encouraging omen is tempered by pain for his enemies' future suffering. That pain is the token of his authentic generosity, not the hollow goodness of a wooden paragon. The pain is *in character*; it is related to other things in Aeneas which hurt him and his mission and which might be regarded as faults. Virgil's nobility lies in his capacity for writing at a high moral level without losing verisimilitude or dramatic intensity. His generosity is spontaneous and human, and so it never dishonestly ignores the cost or the regrets that generosity may involve.

Why has Virgil become so inaccessible? It would appear that the decline of classical education cannot wholly be blamed for his remoteness, since Homer is still read and appreciated in translation. But Virgil in our time has not found his Lattimore, and there is a question whether his poems will ever yield themselves to translation as gracefully as the *Iliad*. It is very hard to understand anything important about Virgil without his language. Perhaps he is also neglected because the *Aeneid,* as a whole, is not so supremely great as the *Iliad,* and thus Virgil seems to run a negligible second best. The comparison with Homer is regrettably unavoidable, because Virgil invited it and built it into his poem, but in fact the *Aeneid* is so different from the Homeric poems that comparisons are often unfruitful. Despite appearances, and despite the author's own conscious intent, the *Aeneid* is unique among epics.

Perhaps the taste for Virgil is unfashionable because he has been identified with the literary Establishment against which the Romantics reacted—as a later generation of rebels reacted in our century. The individual admiration of a Chateaubriand or a Wordsworth—or an Eliot or a Valéry—has not sufficed to obliterate the stigma of neoclassic associations, a stigma intensified by Tennyson's homage. But these historical circumstances would not have sufficed to discredit Virgil did he not fail to supply what we habitually demand from poetry. He is never, for instance, a comic poet; there is a little horseplay in the fifth Aeneid, but not much, and not very funny. He is generally serious, but he is not tragic in any very recognizable fashion—not tragic like Sophocles or Shakespeare. I shall have to speak below of his oblique relation to tragedy. But these wants might be excused if at least the texture of his verse were roughened with irony. Yet here too, alas, he fails. Homer seems closer to the modern world because his ironies are so terrible. When Achilleus taunts the tears of Patroklos who is weeping for his beleaguered comrades, when Achilleus compares him to a little girl, there is a bitter irony for the reader who anticipates Achilleus's own flood of tears for his friend's approaching death. And when, just before his fatal wounding Patroklos taunts his victim Kebriones for the gracefulness of his plunge to death, there is a tragic irony in the fine, gay sarcasm of the doomed victor. Virgil was not given to this Sophoclean cruelty, not, however, because he was ignorant of that complexity in life which irony commonly underscores. Virgil was aware of it, perhaps too aware for the gentleness of his temperament. He was not as *hard* as Homer, and he would have found the Homeric form of tragic irony intolerable. His only form was the straightforward, more bearable sarcasm of Roman oratory, the sarcasm to which Mercury has recourse in his most important epiphany to Aeneas. Before any more generalizations, we ought now to consider that passage.

The gods have frequent occasion to intervene in the action of the *Aeneid*; the superior gods both appear in person (in particular, Venus, Juno, and Apollo) and dispatch emissaries or agents like Iris, Juturna, Opis, and so on. Mercury is dispatched three times by Jupiter—first in book 1 (297ff.), to render Dido hospitable to the storm-weary Trojans, and twice in book 4 (222ff. and 556ff.) to command Aeneas's immediate departure from Carthage. Of all these interventions, only one is described very circumstantially, and only one follows closely the Homeric theme. This is Mercury's second flight. This account is ample; all the others are bare. Virgil may well have chosen to imitate once only this particular convention, and then selected this crux of the narrative in which to do it.

Jupiter's attention is called to Aeneas by his son Iarbas, a Libyan king who has sued unsuccessfully for Dido's hand. Iarbas has heard gossip of Dido's pseudo-"marriage" with Aeneas, an arrangement contrived by Juno with Venus's approbation. Iarbas complains to his father that Dido has yielded to "this second Paris, wearing a Phrygian bonnet to tie up his chin and cover his oily hair, and attended by a train of she-men." This complaint succeeds in turning Jupiter's eyes upon Carthage:

> Talibus orantem dictis arasque tenentem
> audiit Omnipotens, oculosque ad moenia torsit
> regia et oblitos famae melioris amantis.
> tum sic Mercurium adloquitur ac talia mandat:
> "vade age, nate, voca Zephyros et labere pennis
> Dardaniumque ducem, Tyria Karthagine qui nunc
> exspectat fatisque datas non respicit urbes,
> adloquere et celeris defer mea dicta per auras.
> non illum nobis genetrix pulcherrima talem
> promisit Graiumque ideo bis vindicat armis;

sed fore qui gravidam imperiis belloque frementem
Italiam regeret, genus alto a sanguine Teucri
proderet, ac totum sub leges mitteret orbem.
si nulla accendit tantarum gloria rerum
nec super ipse sua molitur laude laborem,
Ascanione pater Romanas invidet arces?
quid struit? aut qua spe inimica in gente moratur
nec prolem Ausoniam et Lavinia respicit arva?
naviget! haec summa est, hic nostri nuntius esto.''

    Dixerat, ille patris magni parere parabat
imperio: et primum pedibus talaria nectit
aurea, quae sublimem alis sive aequora supra
seu terram rapido pariter cum flamine portant.
tum virgam capit: hac animas ille evocat Orco
pallentis, alias sub Tartara tristia mittit,
dat somnos adimitque, et lumina morte resignat.
illa fretus agit ventos et turbida tranat
nubila. iamque volans apicem et latera ardua cernit
Atlantis duri caelum qui vertice fulcit,
Atlantis, cintum adsidue cui nubibus atris
piniferum caput et vento pulsatur et imbri,
nix umeros infusa tegit, tum flumina mento
praecipitant senis, et glacie riget horrida barba.
hic primum paribus nitens Cyllenius alis
constitit: hinc toto praeceps se corpore ad undas
misit avi similis, quae circum litora, circum
piscosos scopulos humilis volat aequora iuxta.
haud aliter terras inter caelumque volabat
litus harenosum ad Libyae, ventosque secabat
materno veniens ab avo Cyllenia proles.
ut primum alatis tetigit magalia plantis,
Aenean fundantem arces ac tecta novantem
conspicit. atque illi stellatus iaspide fulva
ensis erat Tyrioque ardebat murice laena
demissa ex umeris, dives quae munera Dido
fecerat, et tenui telas discreverat auro.
continuo invadit: "tu nunc Karthaginis altae
fundamenta locas pulchramque uxorius urbem
exstruis? heu, regni rerumque oblite tuarum!

> ipse deum tibi me claro demittit Olympo
> regnator, caelum ac terras qui numine torquet:
> ipse haec ferre iubet celeris mandata per auras:
> quid struis? aut qua spe Libycis teris otia terris?
> si te nulla movet tantarum gloria rerum
> nec super ipse tua moliris laude laborem,
> Ascanium surgentem et spes heredis Iuli
> respice, cui regnum Italiae Romanaque tellus
> debetur." tali Cyllenius ore locutus
> mortalis visus medio sermone reliquit
> et procul in tenuem ex oculis evanuit auram.

Such were the words of his prayer, and as he prayed he touched the altar. The Almighty heard, and turned his eyes on the queen's city and on these lovers who had forgotten their nobler fame. He then spoke to Mercury, and entrusted him with this commission: "Up, son of mine, go on your way. Call to you the western winds. Glide on your wings! Speak to the Dardan prince who is now lingering in Tyrian Carthage with never a thought for those other cities which are his by destiny. Go swiftly through the air and take my words to him. It was never for this that the most beautiful goddess, his mother, twice rescued him from his Greek foes. This is not the man she led us to think that he would prove to be. No, he was to guide an Italy which is to be a breeding-ground of leadership and clamorous with noise of war, transmit a lineage from proud Teucer's blood, and subject the whole earth to the rule of law. And even if the glory of this great destiny is powerless to kindle his ardour, and if he will exert no effort to win fame for himself, will he withhold from his son Ascanius the Fortress of Rome? What does he mean to do? What can he gain by lingering among a people who are his foes, without a care for his own descendants, the Italians of the future, and for the lands destined to bear Lavinia's name? He must set sail. That is what I have to say, and that is to be my message to him."

He finished, and Mercury prepared to obey his exalted Father's command. First he laced on his feet those golden sandals with wings to carry him high at the speed of the winds' swift blast over ocean and over land alike. Then he took his wand:

the wand with which he calls the pale souls forth from the
Nether World and sends others down to grim Tartarus, gives
sleep, and takes sleep away, and unseals eyes at death. So
shepherding the winds before him with his wand, he swam
through the murk of the clouds. And now as he flew he
discerned the crest and steep flanks of Atlas the enduring,
who supports the sky upon his head. His pine-clad crown is
perpetually girt by blackest mist and beaten by wind and rain,
his shoulders swathed in a mantle of snow, his aged chin a
cascade of torrents, and his wild and shaggy beard frozen stiff
with ice. Here Cyllenian Mercury first stopped, poised on
balancing wings. And from here he plunged with all his
weight to the waves; like a sea-bird flying low close to the
sea's surface round shores and rocks where fish are found. So
did the Cyllenian fly beneath earth and sky to the sandy shore
of Africa, cutting through the winds from the Mountain At-
las, his mother's sire.

As soon as his winged feet had carried him as far as the
hut-villages of Africa, he saw Aeneas engaged on the foun-
dations of the citadel and the construction of new dwellings.
He had a sword starred with golden-brown jasper, and wore
a cloak of bright Tyrian purple draped from his shoulders, a
present from a wealthy giver, Dido herself, who had made it,
picking out the warp-thread with a line of gold. Mercury
immediately delivered his message: "What, are you siting
foundations for proud Carthage and building here a noble
city? A model husband! For shame! You forget your destiny
and that other kingdom which is to be yours. He who reigns
over all the gods, he who sways all the earth and the sky by
the power of his will, has himself sent me down to you from
glittering Olympus. It is he who commanded me to carry
this message to you swiftly through the air. What do you
mean to do? What can you gain by living at wasteful leisure
in African lands? If the glory of your great destiny is powerless
to kindle your ardour, and if you will exert no effort to win
fame for yourself, at least think of Ascanius, now growing
up, and all that you hope from him as your heir, destined to
rule in an Italy which shall become the Italy of Rome." With
this stern rebuke, and even while he was still speaking, Mer-

cury vanished from mortal vision and melted from sight into
thin air.

(4.219–78)

Virgil's copy of Homer was open as he wrote this passage, but the
innovations he has made in the theme are considerable. Both his in-
debtedness and his originality are most easily studied in the middle
section beginning "Dixerat," a word which is itself a rendering of the
Greek "'H ῥα." The line that follows—"Ille . . . imperio" echoes but
does not follow precisely Homer's formulaic statement of Hermes' obe-
dience. The next three lines, however ("et primum . . . portant"), do
follow word for word Homer's praise of the marvelous sandals. Virgil's
treatment of the staff, in turn, is a significant expansion of Homer's two
lines. Homer had alluded only to the staff's power of inducing and
waking from sleep. Virgil repeats this idea in three words ("dat somnos
adimitque") but chooses to emphasize rather Mercury's role as *psycho-
pompus,* guide to the Lower World—guide both for the newly dead into
that world and for ghosts who are summoned from it. The key phrase
in this sentence is the last—"lumina morte resignat" ("unseals eyes from
death")—which might be applied to either of these duties. We shall want
to consider below the effect of this expansion. Let us note here that the
following line, which ostensibly continues to describe the staff, forms in
fact a transition to the act of flight:

> Illa fretus agit ventos, et turbida tranat
> nubila.

This fine image owes its felicity largely to the juxtaposition of *turbida*
and the verb *tranat* which contains a suggestion of swimming and thus
of effortless, unbroken movement through the swirling clouds.

From this point the passage becomes increasingly Virgilian. The
powerful image of Atlas is original and so is the description of the
overdressed hero, although the simile which separates these two consti-
tutes a modification of Homer's corresponding cormorant simile. Mer-
cury speaks with curt sarcasm and disappears as he concludes, with a
virile abruptness much more Roman than Greek, an abruptness which
will typify the very close of the poem. Mercury's speech is more or less
his own, but it does contain many phrases used by Jupiter ("tantarum
gloria rerum"; "celeris . . . per auras"; "Quid struis, aut qua
spe . . . ?") and one line of his speech (273) is quoted verbatim from

Jupiter's except for the shift to the second person. Virgil remembers but does not imitate Homer's word-for-word repetitions of entire speeches.

All of Virgil's innovations in this passage are made in the same spirit: they introduce a moral dimension into the action while maintaining, or heightening, the grandeur of the god's movement. Virgil is concerned with conferring a certain metaphysical prestige upon right conduct. Aeneas's conduct as the god finds him appears exemplary but is in fact misguided. It represents an evasion, a futile rehearsal of his duty to found the Roman state which was destined to impose order upon the world. Aeneas's evasion stems not so much from any love for Dido as from a dreamy willingness to indulge himself under her opulent, oriental hospitality. Mercury's role as *psychopompus* is relevant because through his descent he is symbolically unsealing the eyes of a man asleep or dead. The instantaneous effect of his epiphany upon Aeneas resembles an awakening or an unsealing of eyes:

> At vero Aeneas aspectu obmutuit amens,
> arrectaeque horrore comae et vox faucibus haesit.

Aeneas was struck dumb by the vision. He was out of his wits, his hair bristled with a shiver of fear, and his voice was checked in his throat.

(4.279–80)

The chthonic associations of Mercury's staff anticipate as well the literal death of Dido, a death which his descent is to bring about. Mercury's mission is actually to send a soul to the Lower World, the "Tartara tristia," even though the allusion in its context seems irrelevant. Aeneas is to encounter Dido as one of the pale shades, the "animas pallentis," when he visits the underworld. Thus the lines devoted to the staff have a twofold reference—to Aeneas and to Dido—even though Virgil leaves their ulterior meaning unstressed.

This transformation of Homeric elements is characteristic of Virgil's procedure throughout. He imitated the episodes and characters and speeches and similes of Greek epic—in particular of Homer—to a point which scandalized some of his early readers. But precisely at those points where he appears most derivative, he is most Virgilian. The broad context of the *Aeneid* metamorphoses the derivative passages and acculturates them to the world of a distinctive, Roman, far more self-conscious imagination. Similes which in the *Iliad* retain a kind of independence from their context, find themselves grafted more firmly and dependently upon the new poem, acquiring now a new moral and symbolic richness. It is a pity that so many of Virgil's imitators during later antiquity and the Renaissance followed his practice but missed the dimension of originality which justified it.

The Virgilian stamp is set upon Mercury's descent partly through the vigorous description of Atlas on which it hinges. The Atlas image is one of those which allows itself most easily to be translated into moral equivalents. There is, to be sure, a slender mythological pretext to justify its appearance, since Atlas was said to be the father of Maia and grand-father of Mercury ("materno veniens ab avo Cyllenia proles"). But the important justification for the image lies in the contrast between Atlas and Aeneas. The great shaggy ice-bound figure sustaining the sky is an *exemplum* of heroic self-denial, of austere exposure to the elements for the sake of the world community. Atlas embodies the qualities which Aeneas has temporarily forgotten. As we first encounter him, Aeneas is exposed to the violence of the elements, enduring as Atlas endures and as the Romans would learn to endure. In the *Aeneid* as in the *Georgics,* the human lot depends upon weather. Only a god like Mercury is master of the elements; as he descends the poet remembers that mastery which is symbolized by the sandals and staff ("quae . . . pariter cum flamine portant"; "illa fretus agit ventos"). But Aeneas, who can only be the victim of the elements, now takes cover from them in Dido's splendid palace. His reprehensible instinct of self-indulgence is visible in the cloak she has given him, the cloak made of Tyrian purple interlaced with golden threads. This cloak and the idle sword, studded ostentatiously with jasper, point the contrast with Atlas's huge battered head. They represent as well Dido's unnatural and possessive hold upon him. Aeneas appears the dandy which Iarbas has scornfully pictured him to be, and this evasive rehearsal at Carthage is an act of cowardice. Thus Mercury's sarcasm:

> Tu nunc Karthaginis altae
> fundamenta locas pulchramque uxorius urbem
> exstruis?

Because of Aeneas's unrelenting servitude to fate, *pulcher* is a word to be used with stinging reproach.

The value placed by the *Odyssey* on beautiful artifacts and on the cultural refinement they manifest is here suspect. There are historical and sociological reasons (as well as reasons private to the poet) why such a shift in values should have occurred. Virgil was writing, not for an audience whose achievement of culture was precarious and thus uncritical, but for an audience whose traditions of austerity were threatened by power, luxury, and corruption. As a result the questions to be posed about Virgil's places are not those viable for his predecessors. In the *Odyssey* one asks "How barbarous or how refined?" In the *Aeneid* one asks "How austere or how decadent?" The beautiful thing was too familiar to be marvelous, as it once had been. The romance of culture had been lost, as Roman eyes were opened to its supposedly insidious seductiveness. The characteristic ritual of the *Odyssey* is the ceremony of hospitality—a ritual of courteous indulgence. But the rituals Virgil admires are the communal habits of work and piety. Dido's brilliant reception of the weary Trojans—with its swirl of ornate gold and silver and fine cloths and music and hecatombs to be feasted on beneath the glowing candelabra and the inlaid ceiling—is a dangerous ritual. It contrasts unfavorably with the simpler hospitality of Pallanteum, where Aeneas spends the night on a pallet of bearskin and leaves.

But if Virgil admired primitive plainness, he did not really admire archaic unrestraint. His primitivism is the backward-looking idealism of a Roman, nothing like the naive serenity in nature of a Homeric Greek. The bird to which Mercury is compared in the *Aeneid*:

> avi similis, quae circum litora, circum
> piscosos scopulos humilis volat aequora iuxta.

is less vivid than the cormorant, its Homeric equivalent, because it has less wild freedom, less rapacity; its genus is not specified—it is simply "a bird," *avis*; moreover, it is a timider bird, haunting the shore rather than crossing seas like the cormorant—and like Mercury. Thus Virgil's bird is less natural and less "real." It is given life by no detail comparable to the salt upon the cormorant's wings. Virgil was not truly at home in the world of untamed nature; he did not feel that fellowship with wild animals which one divines even in those Homeric similes that pit men against animals. He came to the *Aeneid* from writing a great handbook for domesticating natural unruliness.

His largest poem is a handbook for political domesticating—"sub leges mittere orbem." It is a guide as well for the domestication of the self, which also knows its wild beasts. *Empire* is the key idea—empire over the world, over nature and peoples, over language, and over the heart. The respective struggles for command over these various realms imitate and illustrate each other. In the end it is hard to say which *imperium* shows the strictest control—the government of Caesar Augustus, or the hexameters which celebrate it, or the terrible moral discipline which Caesar's ancestor is brought to obey.

II

The character of Aeneas has frequently been criticized, and perhaps most frequently for his conduct after Mercury's descent. The fourth book of the *Aeneid* being its best known (although the second, third, sixth and eighth are at least as fine), Aeneas is remembered as a paragon of deserters, a "master-leaver," to use Enobarbus's phrase. Aeneas is supposed to be unfeeling, wooden, ungrateful, and worse—a cad. The alleged betrayal—the act of a rotter—stands out, and the presentation of his character through the rest of the book, more subtle and understated, counts for less.

Nobody today, I imagine, is going to try to *clear* Aeneas, if only because such an attempt would falsely imply that Aeneas is everywhere admirable. Virgil of course is forever judging his hero, indeed holding up such high standards to judge him by that one is inclined to protest their inhuman strictness. No one will want to absolve Aeneas, but the cliché criticisms, to mean anything, need a context of understanding they do not always receive. First of all, Aeneas's character in book 4 never gets out of hand; it cannot be blamed on the poet's narrative clumsiness or gross moral insensitivity. For better or worse Virgil wants Aeneas to appear as he does. The rest of the poem is there to attest to the powerfully controlling imagination and the almost painfully rigorous moral sense. Virgil has chosen to assign his hero the role of the cad, a little upstage, colorless, and apparently composed, while downstage the heroine tears her passion to magnificent tatters. The Dido drama demonstrates Jackson Knight's remark that "Virgil always sees two sides of everything." He does see them and feel them; that is the reason one can speak of the "painfulness" of his morality. In book 4 he allows one side alone its full pathos, knowing that the weight of the remaining eleven books suffices to right the balance. But such nice artistic calculations are wasted upon the hasty or sentimental reader.

A second qualification to the cliché attacks concerns Aeneas's emotional depth. Whether or not he is in love with Dido—probably he is not—Aeneas is not cold. He would suffer less if he were. The depth of his feelings constitutes the most important thing about him, the thing to start with in speaking of him; it is what makes him interesting and complicated, what leads him to err and disobey, what underlies his nobility. For just as Virgil's nobility is genuine because his generosity is native and human, so the nobility of his hero escapes appearing factitious because it has real emotional substance. Aeneas has dramatic life because his feelings are lifelike; they are impure and fragmentary, confused and intermittent; some of his motives ripen and others wither in the course of the poem. Thus when Mercury leaves him, a malicious reader might find his first response too conventional, too rehearsed:

> At vero Aeneas aspectu obmutuit amens,
> arrectaeque horrore comae et vox faucibus haesit.

but the succeeding line introduces that division of impulses which is the mark of human feeling and above all the mark of Aeneas's feeling:

> ardet abire fuga *dulcisque* relinquere terras

> Already he was ardently wishing to flee from the land of his love and be gone.

> (4.281)

Already in the very phrasing of Mercury's disappearance:

> mortalis visus medio sermone reliquit
> et procul in tenuem ex oculis evanuit auram.

there is a flicker of Virgilian melancholy, of loneliness and regret at the brevity of the gods' apparitions which recalls the more accentuated pathos when Venus leaves Aeneas in book 1. Here in the later scene we know the hero well enough to impute that fleeting regret to his own sensibility although the poet does not explicitly lead us to do so.

Aeneas's emotional intensity is particularly striking in the quality of his religious feeling, that feeling which leads him against his will away from Carthage. His critics tend to discount this strain in him, and yet it is powerfully realized in the poem. Aeneas is not only stolidly pious, in the English sense, or *pius* in the much richer, humane, Latin sense, but he is religious in a more inward way. He is not only punctilious in his duties to the gods and in the divinely-sanctioned duties to those about him. That is his *pietas,* his conscientiousness, but the more remarkable thing about him is the fervor which informs his conscientiousness, a fervor which has no counterpart in the Homeric poems. Aeneas is forever open to a capacity in earthly things for assuming divinity, and he comes to have an intuition of a transcendence in human history. He has occasion in the poem to make several prayers, and in these, curiously, he emerges almost more convincingly and dramatically than anywhere else, as his language becomes most charged and eloquent. Thus the opening of his beautiful prayer to Apollo in the Cumaean cave:

> "Phoebe, gravis Troiae semper miserate labores,
> Dardana qui Paridis derexti tela manusque
> corpus in Aeacidae, magnas obeuntia terras
> tot maria intravi duce te penitusque repostas
> Massylum gentis praetentaque Syrtibus arva:
> iam tandem Italiae fugientis prendimus oras,
> hac Troiana tenus fuerit fortuna secuta."

"Phoebus, you have always pitied Troy in her grievous suffering. It was you who guided the hands of Paris when he aimed his Dardan arrow to strike Achilles the Aeacid. It was you who led me forth to sail over all those seas which thrust against the vast continents and to force a way even to nations of the remote Massylians and lands screened by the Syrtes. Now at the last we have gained a foothold on Italy's elusive shores. From now on, let Troy's old ill-fortune pursue us no farther."

(6.56–62)

Weariness, gratitude, pride, melancholy, faith are mingled here, although translation strains out the poignance of their merging. The prayer exemplifies too that association of Virgilian religion with geography which makes part of its charm, as well as those associations with tradition and festival which the unquoted remainder will introduce.

The charm and beauty of Virgil's religion are actually far more winning in his accounts of human worship, where he is most himself and most spontaneous, than in the heavier, more perfunctory scenes on Olympus, the councils and disputes, where the derivations from Homer are least successful. Virgil's gods, tending as they do to embody abstract principles or forces, court the risk of transparency, and Homeric mystery starts to fade into Virgilian machinery. The descent of Mercury, which lies open to the charge of perfunctory imitation, is saved by those accretions of dramatic meaning we have already noticed. In general, Virgil is at his weakest with his gods, particularly while they remain on Olympus, and this weakness can be attributed to his lack of belief in them as they are thus represented. Virgil's faith must have been like his hero's: inward and intuitive, taking sustenance from places known, from ritual and tradition, from tree and bush and earth. His faith must have been vague in some respects, blurred around the edges, shot with doubts, but his fervor, his openness to some transcendence, were very vital and enriched the dramatic substance of his hero.

It can be granted that Aeneas remains a little muted as a character; he is deep but he is not brilliant. Virgil may well have been incapable of creating a figure as brilliant as the Achilleus of the *Iliad* or the Odysseus of the *Odyssey*. He had no supreme talent for the color and variety of personality. His genius was not quite of that temper, and this is one of the main reasons why he is not to be ranked with Homer, Dante, and Shakespeare. Having granted that, one has then to recognize that Virgil does turn Aeneas's greyness to artistic advantage in the *Aeneid*. For there is an artistic wisdom, as many great writers have discovered, in subordinating the dramatic interest of a protagonist to the interest of those lesser characters he meets and of those events through which he passes. Thus in the *Divine Comedy* the characters of Dante and Virgil acquire their dramatic life much more gradually and subtly than the vivid, spontaneous souls they encounter, and this graduation of revealed drama ultimately lends a firmer, deeper, soberer power to their respective lives within the poem. Thus Mann introduces the protagonist of *The Magic Mountain* by emphasizing his mediocrity, and we come to appreciate the intelligence of his choice of heroes as the macabre story develops. Thus Joyce dismayed Pound by displacing Stephen Dedalus from the center of his novel for a nonentity. Aeneas is not mediocre or simple, but there are places where he is flat, and needs to be flat, if Virgil's emphases are to fall as they should. The *Aeneid* does not hinge so much on personality as upon experience, events, and history. Aeneas's occasional flatness actually helps the reader to lose himself within the hero, to experience what the hero experiences; it is easier to imagine one's self into a neutral character than an eccentric one.

The poem is partly about the moral ambivalences which personality entails. The strongest, most vital personalities in the poem—Dido and Turnus—are defeated and humiliated, while Aeneas comes to succeed only as he gives up his selfhood. He has to surrender the pride and willfulness and energy which his two great victims refuse to surrender and so pay for with their lives. But Aeneas has to surrender still more than that; the deeper selfhood which situates one in a historical and social context, that which gives one a role and makes *pietas* possible. About this deeper kind of identity there are no ambivalences in Virgil's mind: it is the good that makes life possible. When Troy falls, Aeneas loses that identity, that situation in a context, and when he loses it, he tries to die. He is preserved to create another context, another social fabric elsewhere—which he individually is never to enjoy, having created it. He will scarcely have time to descend from his Mount Pisgah. That is his real loss. Troy falls to rise elsewhere, but in him, in his life, it remains fallen. That is why he is so weary, so reluctant, hesitant, and erring, why he lacks the marvelous, Homeric vital energy. He has no place.

It is touching to watch his attempts to reduplicate the fallen city—building his futile Aeneados and Pergamea, envying the miniature Troy of Helenus and the illusory Troy of Dido. Fortunately, perhaps, he does not learn the fullness of his loss all at once, as he gropes through this third book which is so moving and so underestimated. But when after the severest stroke—Anchises' death, Aeneas is swept off-course by the tempest, his *cri de coeur* vents the whole bitterness of his desolation. It is significantly his first speech in the poem, and one of the most brilliant of the Homeric adaptations.

> "o terque quaterque beati,
> quis ante ora patrum Troiae sub moenibus altis
> contigit oppetere! o Danaum fortissime gentis
> Tydide! mene Iliacis occumbere campis
> non potuisse tuaque animam hanc effundere dextra,
> saevus ubi Aeacidae telo iacet Hector, ubi ingens
> Sarpedon, ubi tot Simois correpta sub undis
> scuta virum galeasque et fortia corpora volvit!"

"How fortunate were you, thrice fortunate and more, whose luck it was to die under the high walls of Troy before your parents' eyes! Ah, Diomede, most valiant of Greeks, why did your arm not strike me down and give my spirit freedom in death on the battlefields of Ilium, where lie the mighty Sarpedon, and Hector the Manslayer, pierced by Achilles' lance, and where Simois rolls down submerged beneath his stream those countless shields and helms and all those valiant dead!"

(1.94–101)

The general sense of the first sentence recalls the words of Odysseus in another storm, but the most interesting phrase—*ante ora patrum*—is new. The nostalgia for Troy embraces a nostalgia for the heroic comradeship of Hector and Sarpedon, for such beloved landmarks as the Simois, but most of all for the city of fathers, the city of beloved customs and familial bonds, with a living history of generations and a past flowing into the present. In such a city it is easy to know one's role, and if one's role is to die, even that is relatively easy. One remembers the pathos of Sarpedon's death in the *Iliad*, "far from the land of his fathers"; Aeneas's pathos is to have no land and no father, nor the death which those twin losses bring him to desire.

The nostalgia Aeneas vents at our first sight of him is like a burden of which he has to free himself. He has to stop looking over his shoulder. He is still doing it as book 5 opens: holding his fleet for Italy but looking back at Carthage and the pyre of Dido:

> iam classe tenebat
> certus iter . . .
> moenia respiciens, quae iam infelicis Elissae
> conlucent flammis.

Aeneas and his fleet . . . set course resolutely. . . . As he sailed he looked back to walled Carthage, now aglow with tragic Dido's flames.

(5.1–4)

In the next book, at the Cumaean temple, he pauses to admire the reliefs in which Daedalus has depicted the old stories of Crete, only to earn the sybil's reprimand:

> non hoc ista sibi tempus spectacula poscit
> (6.37)

Not *these* sights do the times demand, but rather such visions of the future as Anchises himself will show his son at the end of the same book. From that experience, Aeneas learns to put his burden down. He has borne it heretofore as he once bore Anchises from the rubble of Troy. He has another burden, the burden of the future, which he now more knowingly shoulders in the latter half of the poem. It is all on the shield which his mother gives him; as he takes it up, pleased though uncomprehending, he bears the glory and destiny of his race.

> attollens umero famamque et fata nepotum.
> (8.731)

Aeneas's identity no longer derives from tradition—Yeats's "spreading laurel tree"—but from the chilly glory of the nation he may not see. He is no longer a son; he must remember he is a father, as Jupiter and

Mercury have urged ("Ascanium surgentem et spes heredis Iuli respice."). The beloved, defeated, human past is exchanged for the bright, metallic future. By the close of the poem, Aeneas is becoming the faceless, official person his new identity requires him to be, the complete and finished *imperium*. His former personality is fast waning, and if in the final brutality, the knifing of Turnus, he reveals a flash of his older impulsiveness, his personal loyalty to Pallas and Evander, he also reveals—the impassivity of the public executioner. The marriage with Lavinia will be the one ritual of his life conducted without feeling. If Aeneas's name is related to the Greek *aineo* (as has been suggested), he becomes at last fully the character his name suggests—"the consenting." Beneath his increasingly effectual activity lies the passivity of acceptance.

No one could possibly be more sensitive to the cost of Aeneas's sacrifice than the poet himself, who hated the violence he felt it necessary to commemorate. It is worth repeating: "He always sees two sides of everything." Just as he allows his hero no moment of indulgence without reproof, so he never allows himself the luxury of the ambivalent. Apparent loss always turns out to be real gain, but so apparent gain turns out—perhaps in spite of him—as profound loss. That is why this poem of celebration and hope reads so often like an elegy. The trees which Virgil praised and loved and imbued with sacred symbolism, the trees which, "rooted in one dear perpetual place," represented that living and growing stability he needed, these—the ashes, oaks, pines, and cedars of the poem—are repeatedly being felled for the pyres of soldiers. Nothing in the *Aeneid* is more elegiac than these litanies of falling timber: for Misenus—

> itur in antiquam silvam, stabula alta ferarum,
> procumbunt piceae, sonat icta securibus ilex
> fraxineaeque trabes cuneis et fissile robur
> scinditur, advolvunt ingentis montibus ornos.

They penetrated into an ancient forest of tall trees where only wild animals lived, and soon spruce-trees were falling, the holm-oak rang under the strokes of the axes, ashen beams and the hard oaks good for splitting were rent apart by wedges, and they rolled down giant rowan-trees from the hills.

(6.179–82)

and later for the dead of the first battle in Italy:

>   pace sequestra
> per silvas Teucri mixtique impune Latini
> erravere iugis. ferro sonat alta bipenni
> fraxinus, evertunt actas ad sidera pinus,
> robora nec cuneis et olentem scindere cedrum
> nec plaustris cessant vectare gementibus ornos.

Peace held the pledges; and Trojans and Latins mingled with-
out hurt as they wandered through woods or on mountain-
slopes. Strokes of the two-edged axe of iron rang on tall ash-
trees. They overthrew pines which towered towards the sky.
Unwearyingly they wedged and split tough oak and scented
cedar; and on groaning wagons they transported rowan-trees.

(11.133–38)

When Troy falls like an ash tree in the great central simile of book 2
(2.624–31), the resonance of its crash never ceases to echo in heartbreak-
ing rhythm. The perpetual elegiac note of the *Aeneid* never turns to
tragic, because tragedy involves the confrontation of loss and the pur-
gation that follows acceptance. Virgil wants always to exalt the loss even
as he winces at it. He denied himself even the luxury of tragedy.

III

I made [elsewhere] a distinction between the poetry of the expected
and of the unexpected, a distinction more or less equivalent to the one
between formulaic and nonformulaic poetry. Now that we are dealing
with work of the far larger second category, it is time to recognize that
it spreads itself out over a broad spectrum. That is to say that all the
verse of literate poets since Homer is not equally unlike his verse in its
degree of what might be called predictability. Accustomed as we are
today to the fireworks of words and images in contemporary poetry,
Virgil and poets like him look almost as far from us as Homer does.
But if we allow for the foreshortening of historical bias, the work of
Virgil and most literate poets writing between about 600 B.C. and
A.D. 1800 (to choose a conservative terminal date) falls into a middle
class flanked on the one hand by formulaic poetry and on the other by
such a figure as Hart Crane. In the poetry of this huge class, you cannot
divine precisely what phrase or image is to follow but the possibilities
are limited; the transitions are not jarring; the images are compliant with
their contexts. A poet like Shakespeare would have to be placed very

close to the moderns upon such a spectrum; a second-rate Petrarchan poet, with his sharply restricted stock of conventional conceits, would belong near the opposite end. Virgil belongs near the center.

At first reading one notices those features of his style which are most conventional and even unpleasantly artificial. Thus, although Virgil's Mercury has no fixed epithet like the Homeric "Argeïphontes"— Argus-Slayer—applied to Hermes, he is called *Cyllenia proles*—Cyllenian scion—with a certain preciosity very far from modern taste. There is a comparable artificiality in Jupiter's allusions to Aeneas as "Dardanium ducem" or to Latium as "Lavinia . . . arva," the Lavinian fields. These circumlocutions are used chiefly in place of proper nouns, but not always; to indicate that Misenus played the trumpet spiritedly, Virgil writes:

> Misenum Aeoliden, quo non praestantior alter
> aere ciere viros Martemque accendere cantu.

> The Aeolid Misenus, who had been excellent beyond all others
> in stirring hearts with his trumpet of bronze and kindling the
> blaze of battle with his music.

(6.164–65)

Aside from this kind of diction, Virgilian language in general looks conservative; for example, he rarely pairs an unexpected adjective with a noun. He makes frequent use of rhetorical tropes like the chiasmus in book 4, line 229:

> gravidam imperiis belloque frementem

tropes which permit the demonic magic in words only a minimum of freedom. Despite this conservatism and these conventional mannerisms, however, Virgil's verbal originality is considerable and appears increasingly greater as one knows him better and knows Latin better. I am not equipped to analyze adequately the subtle mastery of Virgil's style; fortunately Knight's extended treatment is available to obviate an amateur's fumbling [W. F. Jackson Knight, *Roman Vergil*]. But even the reader unable to register with assurance Virgil's artful liberties with syntax and rhythm is likely to feel the warmth and resonance of his poetry, Sainte-Beueve's "calme et puissante douceur," the proud, solemn cadences, the suggestivity, the interpenetration of sound and sense, the powerful organization of large grammatical groups. This impression of broad organization, inevitable to Latin poetry, was heightened by Virgil, who gradually abandoned Catullus's "golden line" for a larger, more complex rhythmic unit—the "verse-group."

The poetic effect of Latin verse is necessarily conditioned by its intricate word order, which differs not only from modern syntax but also from the looser-joined Homeric syntax. A Latin sentence is so dense that it seems not to move in a given linear direction but rather to fill out and form a hypotactic block. A good example is the sentence beginning "Haud aliter . . ." at line 256, where the grammatical subject is delayed till the end, and the place to which ("litus harenosum ad Libyae") precedes the place from which ("materno veniens ab avo"). Reading such a sentence is like watching a photograph come into focus. One gets the impression of weighty materials obedient to their manipulator's will but little impression of movement. Each sentence is a unique little realm governed strictly and not quite effortlessly according to the laws of grammar.

Because its syntax is intricate and hypotactic and its meter so heavily punctuated, Latin poetry tends to render physical movement less well than it renders static situations. I remarked above on the force of the phrase "turbida tranat nubila" (which appears significantly in a short grammatical unit) but I did not add that this is almost the only effective evocation of Mercury's movement. It is followed immediately by the static image of Atlas, and that is followed in turn by the bird simile which does not really succeed in capturing the god's flight. It fails perhaps because the repeated preposition *circum* ("circum litora, circum piscosos scopulos") interferes with the flight's linear direction. This failure to represent movement is typical of Virgil and is compensated for by an ability to render great areas within a single perspective. The poetry of the *Odyssey* is the poetry of a maritime people accustomed to voyage a great deal for military or commercial purposes but without any unifying sense of a single political authority. The poetry of the *Aeneid* is the product of a people who voyage incidentally for administrative purposes and who see any given place as part of a vast whole.

Virgil indeed is a great poet of geography. No epic poet conveys a firmer sense of space, of geographical relationships, and no poet is more sensitive to the coloring with which a man's country imbues him. Consider how many names of peoples and places appear in the episode of Mercury's descent: *Dardanium, Tyria Karthagine, Graium, Italiam, Romanas, Ausoniam, Lavinia*—all these proper nouns in Jupiter's speech alone. Among the finest passages in the great third book are the resonant roll calls of place names. The poet did not in fact travel a very great deal, but he wrote as an imperial Roman, aware of distances and habituated to command vastness. The number of Latin verbs with which spatial prepositions are compounded demonstrates the firm and continuous conception of space in the Roman mind.

Virgil is supreme in his ability to suggest the amplitude of spaces. The concept that the world can be controlled is a powerful motive in the *Aeneid,* as it could not have been before this time and would seldom be again after the fall of the empire. To think that one really controlled the whole vast globe! Jupiter speaks to Mercury of the Roman mission to render all the world subject to law—"totum sub leges mitteret orbem." Virgil's grandeur is manifest in the ease with which his imagination accepted this idea. He does not invade the remote; he contains it. The *Aeneid* is rich in passages which embrace immense space in a phrase or a line of regal simplicity: Dido's allusion to Atlas, for example (enriched as it is by the earlier description we already know):

> "ultimus Aethiopum locus est, ubi maximus Atlas
> axem umero torquet stellis ardentibus aptum."

> "The land of Aethiopia lies on the edge of the world, where giant Atlas holds, turning, on his shoulders the pole of the heavens, inset with blazing stars."
>
> (4.481–82)

or Creusa's prediction to Aeneas:

> "longa tibi exsilia et vastum maris aequor arandum"

> "You have to plough through a great waste of ocean to distant exile."
>
> (2.780)

or the beautiful epitaph for Priam, in which the final proper noun creates a magnificent sense of immensity:

> haec finis Priami fatorum, hic exitus illum
> sorte tulit Troiam incensam et prolapsa videntem
> Pergama, tot quondam populis terrisque superbum
> regnatorem Asiae.

> Priam's destiny ended here, after seeing Troy fired and Troy's walls down; such was the end fated to him who had augustly ruled a great empire of Asian lands and peoples.
>
> (2.554–57)

One kind of image characteristic of Virgil is the broad crowded scene viewed from above. The *Aeneid* contains several of these: Aeneas's view of Troy in flames from his rooftop (2.302–13); the vision of the Elysian souls waiting in their valley to be reborn (6.703ff.); Dido's view of the departing Trojans from her high tower (4.397–411). The fullest of all these images is the first panorama of Carthage as Aeneas sees it from an overlooking hill:

> iamque ascendebant collem, qui plurimus urbi
> imminet adversasque aspectat desuper arces.
> miratur molem Aeneas, magalia quondam,
> miratur portas strepitumque et strata viarum.
> instant ardentes Tyrii: pars ducere muros
> molirique arcem et manibus subvolvere saxa,
> pars optare locum tecto et concludere sulco;
> iura magistratusque legunt sanctumque senatum.
> hic portus alii effodiunt; hic alta theatris
> fundamenta locant alii, immanisque columnas
> rupibus excidunt, scaenis decora alta futuris.

They were now climbing a massive hill which overhung the city and commanded a view of the citadel. Aeneas looked wonderingly at the solid structures springing up where there had once been only African huts, and at the gates, the turmoil, and the paved streets. The Tyrians were hurrying about busily, some tracing a line for the walls and manhandling stones up the slopes as they strained to build their citadel, and others siting some building and marking its outline by ploughing a furrow. And they were making choice of laws, of officers of state, and of councillors to command their respect. At one spot they were excavating the harbour, and at another a party was laying out an area for the deep foundations of a theatre; they were also hewing from quarries mighty pillars to stand tall and handsome beside the stage which was still to be built.

(1.419–29)

There follows the well-known comparison with a hive of bees, just as the view from Dido's tower leads into a comparison with ants. Passages like these are keys to Virgil's conception of history. He tended habitually to discern patterns where other men would see only excrescences, digressions, and eccentricities. There is order in the Carthaginian activity, but no easily grasped order, any more than the pattern of Roman history is easily grasped. The stylistic equivalent of this habit is Virgil's tendency to group in a series elements of various orders of being, as he groups *molem, portas, strepitum,* and *strata* in the passage above. This procedure, resembling as it does the trope of zeugma, gives the effect of reducing diverse things to unity, eliminating particulars for generalities, just as the final two feet of the hexameter, the dactyl and the final firm spondee, cut across the grammatical and word divisions to punctuate the shifting cadences of the first four feet. If such a view of history is taken seriously, then it is easy to see how human beings can be compared to bees or ants.

In many episodes, the *Aeneid* takes this long view of history and the reader too looks down as though from above, almost as though from the throne of Jupiter, to follow the struggling course of progress, with its rhythm of anticipations, correspondences, and recurrences organizing all the variety. The Trojan war itself is incorporated in the synthesis, so that the war in Latium emerges as a reenactment of that earlier war, replacing Hector with Aeneas, Helen with Lavinia, Priam with Evander, and both Achilles and Pyrrhus with Turnus, himself of Greek descent. When Turnus makes his fateful joke:

"Hic etiam inventum Priamo narrabis Achillem."

"You will soon be telling Priam how you have found here a second Achilles."

(9.742)

he is unwittingly echoing the mysterious utterances of the sybil (6.88ff.). Virgil rewrites the *Iliad* to bestow victory on a regenerate Troy, with an implication that the earlier defeat was providential and temporary. By comparable parallels, a vast amount of history and legend is brilliantly made to fit into a network of intermeshed threads.

The difficulty with such Olympian perspectives is that poems cannot be limited to them, and so Virgil has constantly to shift from the grand view to the intimate, from Jupiter making his high prophecies to Aeneas's worries and nostalgias, all the particular roughnesses that destiny ignores. Neither we nor Virgil can help viewing the action from on earth, from the perspective of destiny's victims who cannot take the long view. The sorrow running through the poem has as its source this duality of perspective, which asks us both to pity and accept the suffering which destiny entails.

Few poets have asked so much of their heroes. Of all the celestial descents in the classical epic, none symbolizes so strong a pressure on the human will as Mercury's descent to Aeneas at Carthage. In the *Iliad* the celestial messengers commonly intervene to prompt or suggest, and seldom represent a categorical imperative. Priam can debate with Hekabe whether to follow Iris's admonition; Hermes as a guide is gentleness itself. His descent in the *Odyssey* simply removes an obstacle from the path of the free human will. Apollonius's Eros descends to inflame, actually to weaken the will. But Virgil's Mercury asks that the self be made an *imperium*. Mortality, the great Enemy of the *Iliad,* is very little at issue here, and time is no longer enemy at all, but friend. The true enemy is the unguided human spirit, and the deepest awe is for *its* overcoming.

The corpus of Virgil's poetry possesses a unity which few poets' work attains. In a sense the *Aeneid* requires the *Eclogues* and even more the *Georgics* because it presupposes a quiet reverence for Roman life that modern readers lack. It only gives us glimpses of the felicity which justifies Aeneas's effort. Virgil seems to have taken for granted that his audience would respond to the names of Roman families and ceremonies and places. He assumes that we too love the rivers and trees and farms of Italy, whose serenity justifies centuries of violence. If one does not share that love, even in one's imagination, then one ought to read the earlier poems before returning to the epic. The piety toward family and community, whose *exemplum* is Aeneas, is complemented in the *Georgics* by the pious but pragmatic and unsentimental bond to the soil. One returns to the *Aeneid* grateful for the simpler, sturdier, more cheerful poet, enlivened by a kindliness that tempers duty. That poet has not vanished from his greatest work, but one could wish its bleak nobility to be graced by a mellower, unpremeditated joy. For without that, all empire is as sounding brass.

The Two Voices
of Virgil's *Aeneid*

Adam Parry

I want to begin with the particular. Sometimes we come upon a short passage in a poetic work we know well, a passage we have never particularly noticed before, and all at once, as a kind of epiphany, the essential mood of the author seems to be contained in it. Here is a candidate for such a passage in the *Aeneid*.

There is at the end of book 7 a kind of *Catalogue of Ships,* a muster or roll call of the Latin leaders and their forces as they are arrayed against Aeneas in the long war which occupies the last books of the poem. One of these leaders is a quite obscure figure named Umbro. The Catalogue is an Homeric form, and Virgil here exploits it in the Homeric fashion, drawing out a ringing sense of power from place-names, epithets of landscape and valor, names of heroes. He endeavors further, again in the Homeric fashion, to give individuality within the sense of multitude by singling out some characteristic of each Latin warrior, a device the *Aeneid* has yet more need of than the *Iliad,* since Virgil has behind him no tradition of Latin song which could give the audience a previous familiarity with the heroes he names.

So Umbro comes from the Marruvian people, and he is most valiant: *fortissimus Umbro.* And he is a priest, who possesses the art of shedding sleep over fierce serpents. But—and here we catch the Homeric pathos—his herbs and his incantation could not save *him,* wounded by the Dardanian spear. Virgil then closes the brief scene with a beautiful lamentation:

From *Arion* 2, no. 4 (Winter 1963). © 1963 by the Trustees of Boston University.

For you the grove of Angitia mourned, and Fucinus' glassy waters,
And the clear lakes.

Te nemus Angitiae, vitrea te Fucinus unda,
Te liquidi flevere lacus.

If we could understand wholly the reasons for this lamentation, so elaborate within its brevity, and what makes it so poignant, and why it is so Virgilian, we should, I think, have grasped much of Virgil's art. First, something I can talk about a little but not translate, there is the absolute mastery of rhetoric. We have a *tricolon,* three successive noun-phrases, here in *asyndeton,* that is, with no grammatical connectives, joined to one verb, *flevere, mourned;* and this device combined with *apostrophe*: the dead warrior is suddenly addressed in the second person. The pronoun *te, you,* is repeated thrice, each time in the beginning of one of the three elements of the tricolon, a repetition we call *anaphora.* So much is developed but standard rhetoric. Virgil's mastery consists not in that, but in the subtle variations of it we see here. The three nouns are all a little different. The first is a grove with the name of the goddess to whom it is sacred in the possessive singular: *nemus Angitiae,* the grove of Angitia. The second is the name of a nearby lake, Fucinus, qualified by a noun and adjective: *Fucinus with glassy wave, vitrea Fucinus unda.* The third, beginning another hexameter line, is a common noun *lacus, lakes,* in the plural, with an adjective only: *liquidi lacus, transparent lakes.* The first two nouns are opposed to the third by being names of places. The second and third are opposed to the first by having adjectives and by having adjective and noun separated, whereas *the grove of Angitia, nemus Angitiae,* comes together. But the first and third are also opposed to the second by the variation of the *anaphora*: *te, you,* embodying the directness of lamentation, begins the first phrase: *Te nemus Angitiae. Te* is repeated in the second phrase, but its directness is modulated, softened, by its coming second in the phrase, after the adjective *vitrea, glassy*: *vitrea te Fucinus unda.* Then in the third phrase, the tonic note is struck again: *Te liquidi flevere lacus.* And finally, the verse accent falls on the first *te* and the third, but not on the second:

Te nemus Angitiae, vitrea te Fucinus unda,
Te liquidi flevere lacus.

If this analysis seems too microcosmic, let me say that Virgil may not be, surely is not, the greatest poet who ever lived; but that in this mastery of the disposition of words within a formal pattern, he has no rivals. The effect of the variation within the symmetry is first to establish a rhythm, whose value might finally have to be analyzed in musical terms; and second, to add emotion to the lines. The tricolon with anaphora is a strong formal device, appropriate to the sounds of public lamentation. The variations, like a gentle yielding within the firm tripartite structure, add the note of genuine grief, invest the far-off place names with something of what used to be called the lyric cry.

For it is the place-names in this passage that show us how Virgil has departed from his Homeric model. The Homeric lines the commentators cite here occur in the Catalogue of the Trojans at the end of book 2 of the *Iliad*: "The forces from Mysia were led by Chromius and by Ennomus, a diviner of birds. But his birds did not keep *him* from black death. He was to be slain by the hands of swift Achilles at the river, where many another Trojan fell." The moment of death, and the great slaughter of the Trojans when Achilles returned to battle, is the picture we are left with.

Or again this, from the fifth book of the *Iliad*: "Menelaus son of Atreus caught with his sharp spear Strophius' son Scamandrius, a great hunter. Artemis herself had taught him how to down all the wildlife that the woods nourish. But the huntress goddess Artemis did him no good then, nor did his mastery with the bow for which he was so famous. The son of Atreus, killer Menelaus, struck him with the spear as he fled before him, right between the shoulders, and drove the point out through his chest. And he fell forward, and his armor rang as he fell." Again, and more emphatically in a typical passage such as this, the bitter irony of Homer leaves us with the image of the instant death of the man: the glory of Scamandrius when he lived and was famed as a hunter, then the uselessness of what he was as death comes upon him.

Virgil in the lines about Umbro imitates these scenes. But the image he leaves us with is not a fallen warrior, but a mourning landscape. The dramatic preoccupation of Homer with the single man and the single instant of time gives way to an echoing appeal to the Italian countryside, and an appeal strengthened in wholly un-Homeric fashion by historical associations.

The place-names invoked by Virgil, Marruvium, Lake Fucinus, the grove of the goddess Angitia, are from the Marsian country, hill country to the east of Rome, where a few generations earlier than Virgil a tough and warlike Italian people, the Marsi, had lived in independence, as Roman allies. In the Italian or Marsic war of 91–88 B.C., they had been defeated by Rome, and though they had gained citizenship, they had effectively lost their independence. To Virgil, this people represented the original Italian stock. His feeling for them had something in common with what Americans have felt for the American Indian. They were somehow more Italian than the Romans themselves. Proud, independent, with local traditions hallowed by the names they had given to the countryside, they succumbed inevitably to the expansion of Roman power. The explicit message of the *Aeneid* claims that Rome was a happy reconciliation of the natural virtues of the local Italian peoples and the civilized might of the Trojans who came to found the new city. But the tragic movement of the last books of the poem carries a different suggestion: that the formation of Rome's empire involved the loss of the pristine purity of Italy. Thus the plot of the closing books of the poem centers on Turnus, Aeneas's antagonist, who is made the embodiment of a simple valor and love of honor which cannot survive the complex forces of civilization.

In this light we can understand the form which the lamentation for Umbro takes. Umbro himself is not important. He is no more than a made-up name. The real pathos is for the places that mourn him. They are the true victims of Aeneas's war, and in saying that they weep, Virgil calls on us to weep for what to his mind made an earlier Italy fresh and true.

The lamentation of the ancient hallowed places of the Marsi strikes a characteristic Virgilian note of melancholy and nostalgia, a note produced by the personal accents of sorrow over human and heroic values lost. But equally characteristic is the aesthetic resolution of the lines. The lament is presented to us as an object of artistic contemplation. By this I mean not simply that the lines are beautiful, for that is no distinguishing feature of Virgil. Nor do I refer to the vulgar concepts of "word-painting" or "scenic values," concepts often invoked in Virgilian criticism. The unexpected epithets *vitrea, glassy,* and *liquidi, clear,* do not, I think, "paint a picture" for us. But they do create a sense of sublimation, a conscious feeling that the raw emotions of grief have been subsumed in an artistic finality of vision. Not only the death of Umbro but also the loss of Italy itself is at last replaced by an image of bright and clear waters. The word *vitrea* in the middle of the lamentation is particularly noteworthy, for its connotations are those of an artifact. It is as if Virgil were telling us that the way to resolve our personal sorrow over the losses of history is to regard these losses in the same mood as we would a beautifully wrought vessel of clear glass. The perfection of the lines itself imposes a kind of artistic detachment, and we are put in the position of Aeneas himself, as he sees, in Carthage, the destruction of Troy represented as paintings in a gallery of art.

These paintings remind Aeneas of all that has been, of the *tears of human things*; and at the same time, Virgil tells us, they fill him with hope. In a larger way, the whole poem is such a painting. It is about history, but its purpose is not to tell us that history is good, or for that matter that it is bad. Its purpose is rather to impose on us an attitude that can take into account all in history that is both good and bad, and can regard it with the purer emotions of artistic detachment, so that we are given a higher consolation, and sorrow itself becomes a thing to be desired.

Let us now consider the poem from a wider point of view. Here we take care not to let orthodox interpretations of the *Aeneid* obscure our sense of what it really is. The nostalgia for the heroic and Latin past, the pervasive sadness, the regretful sense of the limitations of human action in a world where you've got to end up on the right side or perish, the frequent elegiac note so apparently uncalled for in a panegyric of Roman greatness—like the passage at the end of book 5 which describes the drowning of the good pilot Palinurus in dark and forgetful waters just before the Trojans reach Italy—the continual opposition of a personal voice which comes to us as if it were Virgil's own to the public voice of Roman success: all this I think is felt by every attentive reader of the poem. But most readers, in making a final judgment on the *Aeneid,* feel nonetheless constrained to put forth a hypothetical "Roman reader" whose eyes were quite unused to the melting mood. *He* would have taken the poem ultimately as a great work of Augustan propaganda, clapped his hands when Aeneas abandons the overemotional Dido, and approved with little qualification the steady march of the Roman state to world dominion and the Principate of Augustus as we see these institutions mirrored in Anchises' speech in book 6 and in Juno's renunciation in book 12. This, we are told, is how we should read the poem. After all, what was Augustus giving Virgil all those gold-pieces for?

So Mr. Kevin Guinach, the Rinehart translator, after putting forth these views, adds: "From this it must not be inferred that Virgil was a hireling. . . . It is fairer to suppose that he was an ardent admirer of the First Citizen and his policies, and sought to promote the reconstruction that Augustus had in mind." Apropos of Dido he says: "The ancient Romans did not read this episode as tearfully as we do. . . . From the Roman point of view, Dido was the aggressor in her marriage to Aeneas, an intolerable assumption of a male prerogative." Moreover, he tells us, the Roman would have condemned her for breaking her vow to her first husband, dead these many years. Consider the case of Vestal Virgins. . . .

But what, on the simple glorification of Rome interpretation, do we make of some of the finest passages of the *Aeneid*? What we find, again and again, is not a sense of triumph, but a sense of loss. Consider the three lines at the end of book 2 which describe Aeneas's attempts to embrace the ghost of his wife:

> Three times I tried to put my arms around her
> And three times her image fled my arms' embrace,
> As light as the winds; as fleeting as a dream.

Like the lines about the fallen warrior, these lines derive from an earlier literary tradition. And again a comparison with this tradition will tell us something about the *Aeneid*. Virgil has two Homeric passages in mind, one in the twenty-third book of the *Iliad* where Achilles tries to embrace the hollow wraith of Patroclus:

> So spoke Achilles, and reached for him, but could not
> seize him, and the spirit went underground, like vapor,
> with a thin cry. And Achilles started awake, in amazement,
> and drove his hands together, and spoke, and his words were
>   sorrowful:
> Ah me! even in the house of Hades there is left something of
>   us,
> a soul and an image, but there is no real heart of life in it!

And a passage from the eleventh book of the *Odyssey,* where Odysseus in the Underworld attempts to embrace the shade of his mother:

> I bit my lip
> rising perplexed, with longing to embrace her,
> and tried three times,
> but she went sifting through my arms, impalpable
> as shadows are, and wavering like a dream.
> And this embittered all the pain I bore.

So the Virgilian passage first of all serves to reinforce the identification, operative throughout the poem, of Aeneas with the heroes of Homer. But the identification only sets in relief the differences. Virgil's lines are characteristic of the whole mood of his poem, the sadness, the loss, the frustration, the sense of the insubstantiality of what could be palpable and satisfying. Virgil emphasizes the *image*—the word *imago* ends the second line; and we can think of countless like passages, such as the appearance of Aeneas's mother in book 1, not recognized until after she has fled. The Homeric heroes are made angry by these signs of what lies beyond our physical existence. Achilles *drives* his hands together, Odysseus is *embittered* that this kind of frustration should be added to his troubles. The Homeric hero, however beleaguered by fate, loves and enjoys the warmth of life, and his course of action includes a protest against the evanescence of mortality. But the sense of emptiness is the very heart of the Virgilian mood. After the three lines I have quoted, Aeneas goes on simply:

> The night was over; I went back to my comrades.

And the third of the three lines

> As light as the winds, as fleeting as a dream

receives a delicate emphasis, partly due to the two different words for *as*

> *Par* levibus ventis, volucrique *simillima* somno

that blurs the contours of our waking senses and gives the line a force of poignant resignation absent from both Homeric passages.

One other passage here, which I will speak of again later on. Aeneas comforts his men after the storm in book 1 with a famous phrase:

> Forsan et haec olim meminisse iuvabit.

> Some day perhaps remembering this too will be a pleasure.

Lifted again from the *Odyssey*. But the Homeric line is quite unmemorable. Odysseus says to his men that some day their troubles now will be a memory. He means only, they will be in the past, don't be overcome by them now. Virgil has made one clear change: the word *iuvabit: it will be a pleasure,* which makes a common-place idea into a profoundly touching one. Not I would insist, because Virgil is a greater poet, but because the kind of sentiment that stands out in the *Aeneid* is different from the kind that stands out in the *Odyssey*.

How much in general is Aeneas like the Greek heroes? We know from the first line that he is cast in the role of Achilles and Odysseus:

> Arms and the man I sing.

The *arms* are of course the *Iliad,* the *man* is the *Odyssey.* And the first six books of the *Aeneid* retrace the wanderings of Odysseus, the wars of the last six books follow the example of the *Iliad.* But the examples are not followed closely. The *Odyssey* goes on after its first line to tell us about the single man Odysseus; the *Iliad* goes on to describe the quarrel that was the first step in the tragedy of Achilles. The *Aeneid* moves from Aeneas straightway to something larger than himself: Rome:

> that man who was tossed about on land and sea
> and suffered much in war until
> he built his city, brought the gods to Latium
> from whence the Alban Fathers, the towering walls of Rome.

Aeneas from the start is absorbed in his own destiny, a destiny which does not ultimately relate to him, but to something later, larger, and less personal: the high walls of Rome, stony and grand, the Augustan Empire. And throughout he has no choice. Aeneas never asserts himself like Odysseus. He is always the victim of forces greater than himself, and the one lesson he must learn is, not to resist them. The second book of the poem drills him thoroughly in this lesson. The word Aeneas keeps using, as he tells of the night Troy fell, is *obstipui*: I was *dumbfounded,* shocked into silence. Again and again he tries to assert himself, to act as a hero, and again and again he fails. He leads a band of desperate Trojans against the Greeks, but it all turns sour. The Trojans dress up as Greeks, an unheroic stratagem which works for a while, but then their own countrymen mistake them, and Trojans slaughter each other, while Aeneas himself ends up on the roof of Priam's palace, passive spectator of the terrible violations within. A key passage is the one in which Aeneas is about to kill Helen. At least the personal, if not entirely heroic, emotion of revenge can be satisfied. But his mother stops him, not with a personal plea, as Athena checks Achilles in the *Iliad,* but by revealing for an instant the gods at work destroying the city. Against such overwhelming forces as these, individual feeling has no place. Aeneas must do the *right* thing, the thing destiny demands, and sneak away from Troy.

One of the effects, then, of the epic identifications of Aeneas is ironic contrast: he is cast in a role which it is his tragedy not to be able to fulfill. Let us now consider another kind of identification: the historical ones. As well as being cast as Odysseus and Achilles, Aeneas has to be the emperor Augustus. Of many passages, this one in the third book particularly contributes to setting up the connection. Aeneas and his men coast along the western shore of Greece and stop at Actium, where there is a temple of Apollo. There they hold games and Aeneas fastens to the door of the temple spoils taken from the Greeks with the inscription THESE ARMS FROM THE GREEK VICTORS. The reason for this action in this place is that Augustus had won his great victory over Antony and Cleopatra a few years earlier at Actium. He had instituted games in honor of his victory, and he liked to identify himself with Apollo. Moreover THE GREEK VICTORS, who are now vanquished, represent the armies of Antony, who recruited his forces from the eastern Mediterranean, whereas Augustus made himself the champion of Italy. So that the victory Aeneas somewhat illogically claims here by dedicating Greek spoils prefigures the victory that was to establish the power of Augustus.

Some striking verbal parallels confirm the connection; and give us as well insight into Virgil's technique. At the beginning of book 3, Aeneas sets sail from Troy.

> I am borne forth an exile onto the high seas
> With my comrades, my son, the Penates and the Great Gods

> Cum sociis natoque Penatibus et Magnis Dis.

The exact meaning of the phrase *the Penates and the Great Gods* is obscure. But it is clear that they are some sort of cult statues of Troy, destined to become cult statues of the New Troy, or Rome. The oddity of the phrase in fact helps us to remember it—the Romans liked their religious language to be obscure—and so does its remarkable thudding rhythm: *Penatibus et Magnis Dis*. This is Aeneas in his sacral character as bearer of the divine charter of Troy.

At the end of book 8, Vulcan makes a shield for Aeneas, and on it are engraved scenes from subsequent Roman history. One of these scenes depicts the Battle of Actium:

> On one side stands Augustus Caesar leading Italians into
>   battle,
> With the Fathers (i.e., the Senate), the People, the Penates and
>   the Great Gods

> Cum patribus populoque, Penatibus et Magnis Dis.

Aeneas's shield shows the future version of himself.

But Aeneas is not just Augustus. There is also the possibility of his being Augustus's bitter enemy, Mark Antony. Such is the identification we are led to make when, in the fourth book, he has become the consort of Dido, queen of Carthage. Thus the contemptuous description of him by Iarbas, his rival for Dido's love, "that Paris with his effeminate retinue," closely matches the image of Antony and Cleopatra with their corrupt eastern armies which Augustus created for Roman morale.

And Dido is Cleopatra. When she is about to die, she is said to be *pale with imminent death, pallida morte futura*. Cleopatra, in her own person, is described on Aeneas's shield in book 8 as *paling before imminent death, pallentem morte futura*.

To understand the meaning in the poem of these historical identifications, we must first consider more fully the figure of Aeneas. We learn from the second line of the poem that he is a man *exiled by fate, fato profugus,* and we soon learn that fate has for Aeneas implications that go beyond his personal journey through life. He is a man blessed—or is it cursed?—with a mission. The mission is no less than to be the founder of the most powerful state known to history; and so his every act and his every passion, all that he does, all that he feels and all that happens to him is in the light or under the shadow of this immense prophetic future of which he, by no choice of his own, is the representative elected by the gods. Every experience he passes through, therefore, has a significance greater than the events of an ordinary man's life could possibily have. Every place he visits acquires an eternal fame of one kind or another. Every action he performs, every word he speaks, is fraught with consequences of which he himself can only dimly perceive the enormity.

This sense of pregnant greatness in every detail of experience is impressed on us too by the rhetorical exaggeration which pervades the *Aeneid,* and by the unrealism of many of its incidents. Juno's wrath in book 1 is magnified far beyond Poseidon's resentment in the *Odyssey*; Athena's punishment of the lesser Ajax, which Juno would like to inflict upon Aeneas, is enlarged into a cosmic destruction. When there are storms, the waves rise up and lash the heavens. Dido is supposed to have arrived in Africa not long before with a small band of refugees; but already the construction of a tremendous city—the later Carthage, of course—can be seen, complete with temples and art-galleries. Aeneas is moving through a world where everything is a symbol of something larger than itself. The layers of literary and historical allusion reinforce this sense of expansion in space and time which every monumental hexameter verse imposes on the reader.

The potentialities of ages and empires are alive in the smallest details of the *Aeneid,* and Aeneas has been made into the keystone of it all. The inconceivable destiny of Rome rests upon his shoulders. The *Aeneid* can give a literal meaning to that cliché. So line 32 of the first book:

Tantae molis erat Romanam condere gentem

It was a thing of so much *weight* to found the Roman race.

Aeneas can only leave Troy by carrying his aged father upon his shoulders. And Anchises is more than Aeneas's father. He is the burden of destiny itself. Thus in book 6 it is he who unfolds the panorama of Roman history to his son who has descended to the Nether World to hear him. And at the end of book 8, Virgil insists on Aeneas's role as bearer of destiny. The shield which Vulcan makes for him corresponds to the one he made for Achilles in the *Iliad*. Only Achilles' shield was adorned with generic pictures of life: a city at peace, a city at war, a scene of harvest, a scene of dancing, and so on. Aeneas's shield is adorned with scenes from Roman history, history which is future to him—it is here that we read of Augustus at the Battle of Actium—and as he puts it on, Virgil says:

He marvels at the scenes, events unknown to him,
And lays upon his shoulder the fame and fate of his descendants

Attollens umero famamque et fata nepotum.

The burden may well be a heavy one to bear, particularly if the bearer of it himself is permitted only an occasional prophetic glimpse into its meaning. And when such a glimpse is permitted him, it is likely to be anything but reassuring.

Bella, horrida bella

Wars, hideous wars! the Sibyl shrieks at him when he questions her in book 6. "You will get to Latium, all right," she tells him, "but you will wish you had never come!" *Sed non et venisse volent.* "Go, seek your Italy!" Dido tells him, and then prophesies: "Let him beg for help in his own land, and when he has accepted the terms of a shameful peace, let him not enjoy his realm, or that light he has prayed for, but

fall before his time, and lie unburied on the sands

Sed cadat ante diem mediaque inhumatus harena,

whereby Aeneas is included in an almost obsessively recurrent series of images of disgraceful and nameless death.

Labor, ignorance and suffering are Aeneas's most faithful companions on his journey to Rome. And at once to intensify his own suffering and lack of fulfillment and to magnify the destiny he is serving, Aeneas must witness the happiness and success of others. In the third book he visits his kinsman Helenus in Epirus, and there he sees a copy of Troy, laid out in miniature. Aeneas is at first hopeful as he asks the prophetic Helenus for advice: "Now tell me, for I have divine sanction for all I do, and the gods have promised me a happy course, tell me the labors I must undergo, and the dangers I must avoid." But a little later, when Anchises enters, and he must set sail again, Aeneas falls into despair: "May you live happy, for your destiny is accomplished; but we are called from one fate to another . . . You have peace, you have no need to plow up the sea and follow forever the forever receding shores of Italy."

> Arva neque Ausoniae semper cedentia retro
> Quaerenda.

What this and other like passages impress upon us is something subtly at variance with the stated theme of the poem. Instead of an arduous but certain journey to a fixed and glorious goal, there arises, and gathers strength, a suggestion that the true end of the Trojan and Roman labors will never arrive. It is not that Aeneas will literally never arrive in Latium, found a city, and win his wars. That is as certain as it is that Odysseus will return to Ithaca. But everything in the *Odyssey* prepares us for a fuller end to Odysseus's labors: we are made always to expect his reinstatement in kingship, home, honor and happiness. In the *Aeneid* every prophecy and every episode prepares us for the contrary: Aeneas's end, it is suggested, will see him as far from his fulfillment as his beginning. This other Italy will never cease receding into the distance.

There is another dimension to Aeneas's suffering as the bearer of too vast a destiny. Aeneas cannot live his own life. An agent of powers at once high and impersonal, he is successively denied all the attributes of a hero, and even of a man. His every utterance perforce contains a note of history, rather than of individuality. He cannot be himself, because he is wired for sound for all the centuries to come, a fact that is reflected in the speeches of the *Aeneid*. The sonorous lines tend to come out as perfect epigrams, ready to be lifted out of their context and applied to an indefinite number of parallel situations. Aeneas arrives in Carthage and sees the busy construction of the city.

O fortunate you, whose walls already rise!

he cries out.

O fortunati, quorum iam moenia surgunt!

That line is memorable, too memorable perhaps for spontaneity. What Virgil has done is to turn to peculiar account what is at once the weakness and the glory of much of Latin verse: its monumentality, and its concomitant lack of dramatic illusion.

But Aeneas's failure as a hero goes deeper than the formality of his speech. As he makes his way through the first six books, we see him successively divested of every personal quality which makes a man into a hero. We have seen how the weight of his mission is made to overwhelm him at the very beginning of the poem. In the second book, he is in a situation which above all calls for self-sacrifice in the heat of battle. But this is precisely what he is kept from doing. Hector appears to him in a dream and tells him not to die for his country, but to flee. "For if Troy could have been saved," the ghost says almost with condescension, "my right arm would have saved it." We understand that Aeneas's words in the first book, when he was overwhelmed by the storm, have a deeper meaning than the parallel lines of the *Odyssey*: "O thrice and four times happy, you who fell at Troy!" Odysseus spoke out of a momentary despair. Aeneas's words are true for all his life. His personal ties too are not kept intact: in his haste to get his father and the state gods out of Troy, he leaves his wife behind; and when he returns to fetch her, she is an empty phantom, who can comfort him only with another prophecy.

But the most dramatic episode and the one in which Aeneas most loses his claims to heroism is the fourth book. The tragedy of Dido is lucid and deeply moving. But the judgment it leads us to make on Aeneas needs some comment. Generations of Latin teachers have felt it necessary to defend Aeneas from the charge of having been a cad. Modern readers are romantic, but a Roman reader would have known that Aeneas did the right thing. So the student is asked to forsake his own experience of the poem for that of a hypothetical Roman. Another theory is that Virgil somehow fell in love with, and was carried away by, his own heroine. But we cannot explain Virgil by assuming that he did not intend to write as he did. It is clear that on the contrary Virgil deliberately presented Dido as a heroine, and Aeneas as an inglorious deserter. Dido's speeches are passionate, and, in their operatic way, ring utterly true. Aeneas can apologize only by urging that his will is not his own. "If I had had my way," he tells her, "I would never have left Troy to come here at all." "I would never have fallen in love with you in the first place," he seems to mean. "I follow Italy not of my own choice." *Italiam non sponte sequor.* Of course he is right. Aeneas's will is not his own, and the episode in Carthage is his last attempt to assert himself as an individual and not as the agent of an institution. And in his failure, he loses his claim even to the humbler of the heroic virtues. For piety, in the Roman sense, meant devotion to persons as well as the state. "Unhappy Dido!" the queen about to die cries out, "is it now his impious deeds become clear to you? They should have before, when you made him your partner in rule. See now his pledge of faith, this man who carries about his gods, and his ancient father on his back." For pious Aeneas, as he is called, and calls himself, throughout, cannot maintain even his piety in a personal way.

Two later passages serve to emphasize this. At the beginning of the fifth book, the Trojans sail to Italy, troubled by the death-fires they see back in Carthage. "For they knew what a woman is capable of, when insane with the grief of her love dishonored." The Latin is perhaps more blunt. Dido's love was literally *defiled, polluto amore,* and Aeneas is its defiler. Later, in the Underworld in book 6, Aeneas meets Dido. He wants reconciliation now, and begs forgiveness. "I did not know the strength of your love for me," he says. Again the implication is clear. Aeneas did not know, because he could not feel the same love for her; because he is not master of himself, but the servant of an abstract destiny. Dido, speechless in anger, turns away. Aeneas is modelled on Odysseus here, and Dido's shade is the shade of Ajax in book 11 of the *Odyssey.* Virgil strengthens the emotions this scene creates in us by recalling the one scene in the *Odyssey* where Odysseus meets a hero greater than himself, and is put to shame by his silence.

But Dido, we remember, is also Cleopatra, and we must consider the meaning of that identification. Dido-Cleopatra is the sworn enemy of Rome:

Rise thou forth from my bones, some avenger!

Exoriare aliquis nostris ex ossibus ultor!

invoking the fell shades of Hannibal; but she is a tragic heroine. Aeneas, on the other hand, could have been, and for a while seemed to be, Antony, losing a world for love. Only he must in the end be Augustus, losing love and honor for a dubious world. The *Aeneid,* the supposed panegyric of Augustus and great propaganda-piece of the new regime, has turned into something quite different. The processes of history are presented as inevitable, as indeed they are, but the value of what they achieve is cast into doubt. Virgil continually insists on the public glory of the Roman achievement, the establishment of peace and order and civilization, that *dominion without end* which Jupiter tells Venus he has given the Romans:

Imperium sine fine dedi.

But he insists equally on the terrible price one must pay for this glory. More than blood, sweat and tears, something more precious is continually being lost by the necessary process; human freedom, love, personal loyalty, all the qualities which the heroes of Homer represent, are lost in the service of what is grand, monumental and impersonal: the Roman State.

The sixth book sets the seal on Aeneas's renunciation of himself. What gives it a depth so much greater than the corresponding book of the *Odyssey* is the unmistakable impression we have that Aeneas has not only gone into the Underworld: he has in some way himself died. He descends carrying the Golden Bough, a symbol of splendor and lifelessness. The bough glitters and it *crackles in the wind*:

sic leni crepitabat brattea vento.

It sheds, Virgil says, a strange discolored aura of gold; and it is compared to the mistletoe, a *parasitic plant, quod non sua seminat arbos,* a plant with no vital connection to the tree to which it clings. A powerful contrast to the culminating image of the *Odyssey,* that great hidden rooted tree from which the bed-chamber, the house and the kingship of Odysseus draw continuous and organic life.

Aeneas moves through the world of the dead. He listens, again the passive spectator, to the famous Roman policy speech of Anchises, a speech full of eagles and trumpets and a speech renouncing the very things Virgil as a man prized most:

Let others fashion the lifelike image from bronze and marble;
Let others have the palm of eloquence;
Let others describe the wheeling constellations of heaven;
Thy duty, O Roman, is to rule

Tu regere imperio populos, Romane, memento

When he emerges, so strangely, from the ivory gate of false dreams, he is no longer a living man, but one who has at last understood his mission, and become identified with it. Peace and order are to be had, but Aeneas will not enjoy them, for their price is life itself.

And yet there is something left which is deeper than all this. It is the capacity of the human being to suffer. We hear two distinct voices in the *Aeneid,* a public voice of triumph, and a private voice of regret. The private voice, the personal emotions of a man, is never allowed to motivate action. But it is nonetheless everywhere present. For Aeneas, after all, is something more than an Odysseus manqué, or a prototype of Augustus and myriads of Roman leaders. He is man himself; not man as the brilliant free agent of Homer's world, but man of a later stage in civilization, man in a metropolitan and imperial world, man in a world where the State is supreme. He cannot resist the forces of history, or even deny them; but he can be capable of human suffering, and this is where the personal voice asserts itself.

Someday these things too will be pleasant to think back on

Forsan et haec olim meminisse iuvabit

he tells his comrades in book 1. The implication is that when the great abstract goal is finally somehow reached, these present sufferings, seen in retrospect, will be more precious than it.

And so this pleasure, the only true pleasure left to Aeneas in a life of betrayals of the self, is envisaged as art. The sufferings of the Trojans, as Aeneas sees them in Carthage, have become fixed in art, literally: they are paintings. And it is here first, Virgil tells us, that Aeneas began to hope for a kind of salvation. Here he can look back on his own losses, and see them as made beautiful and given universal meaning because human art has transfigured them. "Look here!" he cries. "There is Priam; there are tears for suffering, and the limitations of life can touch the heart."

Sunt lacrimae rerum et mentem mortalia tangunt.

The pleasure felt here by Aeneas in the midst of his reawakened grief is the essential paradox and the great human insight of the *Aeneid,* a poem as much about the *imperium* of art as about the *imperium* of Rome. The images in Carthage make Aeneas feel Priam's death not less deeply, but more. At the same time they are a redemption of past suffering, partly because they remove one element of the nightmare: final obscurity and namelessness, partly because they mean that we have found a form in which we can see suffering itself clearly. The brightness of the image and the power of pleasurable vision it confers, consoles for the pain of what it represents.

The pleasure of art in fact gives value to the pain itself, because tragic experience is the content of this art. Virgil continues the scene in the art-gallery: "He spoke, and with deep sorrow, and many lamentations, fed his soul on the empty pictures."

> Atque animum pictura pascit inani.

Empty—*inani*—is the key-word here. Consider again how many times Virgil creates his most touching scenes by dwelling on how something substantial becomes empty and insubstantial: the phantom of Creusa, old fallen Troy, the apparition of Venus in book 1, the shade of Dido in the Underworld, the lost pledge to Evander, the outraged life of Turnus. *Inanis* is the very word that describes the tears Aeneas sheds upon leaving Carthage and Dido: "His mind was unmoved; the tears he wept were empty." That is, *of no avail*.

> Mens immota manet; lacrimae volvuntur inanes.

Aeneas's tragedy is that he cannot be a hero, being in the service of an impersonal power. What saves him as a man is that all the glory of the solid achievement which he is serving, all the satisfaction of "having arrived" in Italy means less to him than his own sense of personal loss. The *Aeneid* enforces the fine paradox that all the wonders of the most powerful institution the world has ever known are not necessarily of greater importance than the emptiness of human suffering.

Depths and Surfaces

W. R. Johnson

The inner image of the verse is inseparable from the numberless changes of expression which flit across the face of the teller of tales as he talks excitedly.
—MANDELSTAM

In reading Virgil, I often cry: "Out hyperbolical fiend! How vexest thou this man!"
—HOUSMAN to Mackail (1920)

novae cacozeliae repertor
—*Vita Donati*

After sketching a quick, sure portrait of the melancholy Victorian Virgil, R. D. Williams issues this shrewd and timely warning: "The twentieth-century critic, immersed in this pool of tears, may well look longingly for a dose of the hard and robust Dryden, asking to be allowed to disinvolve himself, to be permitted a little distance. And this surely is what Virgil gives him, provided that he does not substitute for the *Aeneid* an anthology of the most intense parts of the second, fourth, sixth, and twelfth books." As I look over the passages chosen for discussion in this [essay] and the way I have organized those passages, I realize, with some chagrin, that I have been busily constructing the forbidden anthology. But the portrait that emerges from the following pages bears no resemblance to the portrait that Williams correctly designs from the Victorian (and later) readings of this kind. In examining Virgil's style and narrative structure in these "intense parts" of the books in question, in looking

From *Darkness Visible: A Study of Vergil's* Aeneid. © 1976 by the Regents of the University of California. University of California Press.

at Virgil's concern with *nescius, vacuus, umbra, imago, res,* I have found strong traces of—and have chosen to emphasize—the harsher aspects of Virgilian "unreality" and "deliberate confusedness," a bitterness in the famous lyricism that borders on despair—in other words, the muscle beneath the "softer emotional mode" that is strained almost beyond its limit in a fateful and unequal struggle against madness, anger, profound ignorance, vulnerability, and malevolent darkness. In choosing to emphasize these qualities of Virgilian poetic I am not denying the existence or the importance of wistful lyricism or melancholy lustre or tender humanism; still less am I seeking to pretend that the tough and dynamic aspects of Virgil's art which Williams stresses so strongly and brilliantly do not exist. What I want to investigate here are the dark places of Virgil's impressionism and the mordancy of the stiff, almost expressionistic gestures of his language and narrative, for these parts of Virgil's poetic have not yet, I think, received the attention they merit. And until we have a clear notion of the forms these poetic modes may take, we are apt to mistake them for modes that are deceptively similar to them. Specifically, what interests me most [here] is what I call the negative image: what it is, what it looks like, how Virgil goes about shaping it, and, finally, the kinds of things it tends to signify.

I. The Opening of Book 12

at regina nova pugnae conterrita sorte,
flebat, et ardentem generum moritura tenebat,
"Turne, per has ego te lacrimas, per si quis Amatae
tangit honos animum, spes tu nunc una, senectae
tu requies miserae; decus imperiumque Latini
te penes; in te omnis domus inclinata recumbit:
unum oro: desiste manum committere Teucris.
qui te cumque manent isto certamine casus,
et me, Turne, manent; simul haec invisa relinquam
lumina, nec generum Aenean captiva videbo."
accepit vocem lacrimis Lavinia matris
flagrantes perfusa genas, cui plurimus ignem
subiecit rubor, et calefacta per ora cucurrit.
Indum sanguineo veluti violaverit ostro
si quis ebur, aut mixta rubent ubi lilia multa
alba rosa; tales virgo dabat ore colores.

illum turbat amor, figitque in virgine vultus:
ardet in arma magis paucisque adfatur Amatam.

But frightened by the terms of this new duel,
the queen, weeping, prepared to die, held fast
her raging son-in-law: "Turnus, by these
tears and by any reverence you still
feel for Amata—you, the only hope
and quiet left my sad last years: the honor
and power of Latinus is with you,
this house in peril stands or falls with you;
I beg one thing: you must not meet the Trojans.
For in this duel that you so wish to enter,
whatever waits for you waits for me, too;
together with you, I shall leave this hated
light; for I will not be a captive, see
Aeneas as my son-in-law." Lavinia's
hot cheeks were bathed in tears; she heard her mother's
words; and her blush, a kindled fire, crossed
her burning face. And just as when a craftsman
stains Indian ivory with blood-red purple,
or when white lilies, mixed with many roses,
blush: even such, the colors of the virgin.
His love drives Turnus wild; he stares at his
Lavinia; even keener now for battle,
he answers Queen Amata with few words.
        [12.54–71; Allen Mandelbaum, tr. (Berkeley and
        Los Angeles: University of California Press,
        1971); all further translations in this essay of the
        Aeneid are from this edition.]

At the opening of book 12 Turnus confronts Latinus and reaffirms his decision to fight Aeneas in single combat. Latinus, torn by bad conscience since he knows what Fate has commanded and knows, too, that he has been impotent to fulfill those commands, begs Turnus to desist from his plan and to submit to the will of Heaven, both for the good of the Latins and for his own good. Latinus's passionate plea fades with a skillful compressed echo of *Iliad* 22.38–76, Priam's shrewd appeal to filial love:

> misere parentis
> longaevi, quem nunc maestum patria Ardea longe
> dividit.

> Pity your aged father: even now his native
> Ardea holds him far from us, in sadness.
>
> (12.43–45)

So, far from convincing Turnus to yield to the inevitable, Latinus's common sense and his concern serve only to inflame Turnus the more:

> haudquaquam dictis violentia Turni
> flectitur; exsuperat magis aegrescitque medendo.

> Words cannot check the violence of Turnus:
> the healing only aggravates his sickness;
> his fury flares.
>
> (12.45–46)

The oxymoron ("he sickens because of the cure") emphasizes Turnus's irrationality (this is the second use of *violentia* in this scene: *haud secus accenso gliscit Turno* [9]) even as it illumines much of what is strange about the opening scene as a whole. If *aegrescitque medendo* corresponds to anything in its Homeric model in *Iliad* 22, it can only be to the two occurrences of *oud' Hektori thumon epeithon* (78 and 91). The spare precision of Homer's phrase gains force with repetition (neither Priam nor Hecuba can change Hector's *thumos* with their separate pleas), and its lack of imagery brings into clear focus the heightened imagery of sickness with which Virgil chooses to complete the confrontation of Turnus and Latinus. It is not enough to say that Virgil desires to show by his oxymoron the wide difference between Turnus's state of mind and that of Hector (Turnus's unbridled passion as against Hector's controlled excitement and resolve: *amoton memaōs Achilēi machesthai* [36]) in order to emphasize, by this artful contrast, the full force of Turnus's *violentia*. The chief function of the oxymoronic metaphor is to dissolve the outlines of a scene that never quite gets under way. As we move from Turnus's second outburst to Amata's outburst, to Lavinia's blush, and, finally, to Turnus's third and last speech, we sense that Latinus's gesture is, like all of his gestures, futile: not because it is in itself unreasonable, but because Turnus suffers from an irrational sickness that is beyond this help or any help.

In the case of Hector, the fact that both Priam and Hecuba fail to persuade their son to desist from his resolve does not mean that persuasion could not possibly work in this instance; it means only that it happens not to work in this instance because both Fate and Hector's own character are more powerful even than the cunning, honest, and elemental rhetoric of his parents. Homer's world in this scene, as in his other scenes, is the common world where health and rational discourse are the norm from which sickness and irrationality deviate. In this world the outlines of events and the motives of the human beings who participate in those events are generally extremely clear. Priam and Hecuba know what they are doing, and what they are doing is reasonable. Hector knows what he is doing, and his choices and behavior are at once utterly rational and utterly honorable. But the motives, the behavior, and even the dilemmas of Turnus are far less clear than are those of Hector.

Virgil cannot present them with the clear outlines and exact articulations that Homer uses for his scene because Turnus is sick, as Virgil emphasizes with his powerful oxymoron, and because the causes of this sickness (and indeed the fact of the sickness itself) are unknown to Turnus himself, to Latinus, to Amata, and even, in a way, to Virgil and to us. The sickness that destroys Turnus, that is in some ways the central concern of book 12 and therefore in some ways the central concern of the epic as a whole, is not susceptible to rational analysis and is therefore not susceptible to firm design and the sequential clarity that are the hallmarks of Homer's mode of beholding. Virgil will not, or, as I propose, cannot show us what Turnus suffers and does in this scene. Rather, what he does is to suggest the emotions that Turnus unconsciously suffers while under the illusion that he is performing a conscious, rational act. In saying this I do not mean to suggest that what Virgil offers us here is a psychological analysis of Turnus; that he is, to use another metaphor, being subjective rather than objective; or, to alter the same metaphor slightly, that he is turning from the outward appearance to the inward reality.

What Virgil offers here are clusters (not a series or groups) of blurred images that suggest but do not and cannot try to define the fluctuations and uncertainties of Turnus's distorted perceptions; what Virgil offers are not inner realities, but illusions. The fact that these perceptions are distorted from the outset (from, say, the moment when Allecto's magic firebrand becomes a real torment that really drives Turnus mad) means that they can never crystallize for him and for us into a true conception of who he is or what he is up against. Thus, whereas Hector has a fairly good understanding of the fate he moves toward inevitably and of why he confronts it, why he must confront it, Turnus gropes in blind frenzy to a death that is finally terrible and unredeemed (Hector's, as I shall try to show, is, essentially, redeemed) in exact proportion as it is finally hellish and incomprehensible. Both for Turnus's "point of view" in this scene, then, and for Virgil's own mode of beholding at crucial moments throughout his epic, the image of sickness as madness is, perhaps paradoxically, exact, and it shows "a clearness of the unclear" that is, to my mind, a prime characteristic of Virgil's art. But for our present purposes, I wish to emphasize that the oxymoron stresses, by its twisted graphic antithesis, the essential futility of the interview between Turnus and Latinus: the diseased irrationality that is *violentia* has grown to such proportions that its virulence feeds on what should cure it. In its striving to suggest the nature and degree of Turnus's *violentia,* the oxymoron signals that there can be no further dramatization of Turnus's inner conflicts, and it dissolves such drama and reality as have been faintly sketched just before it. At this point we realize that Turnus, now so fully identified with his madness as to be indistinguishable from it, can neither speak to the issue with Latinus nor can Latinus speak to him; he is, in a very real sense, a phantom wandering through the broken images that constitute his delusions, his consciousness.

In this regard, it is useful to contrast the general outline of the scene with its Homeric counterpart. Book 22 opens, as book 21 has ended, with the routed Trojans trampling one another in their efforts to get inside the walls of the city. Apollo, who has disguised himself as Agenor and so led Achilles on a wild-goose chase, mocks his victim and meets with an angry, defiant response from him; then Achilles wheels around and rushes back to the city. He is immediately seen by Priam, who is on the ramparts and who immediately begins to beg Hector to retire inside the walls. The setting for the first main action of the book, the parents' entreaties to the doomed warrior, is sketched with quick and characteristic economy and clarity. The transition between book 11 and 12 of the *Aeneid* is less directly handled than is that between books 21 and 22 of the *Iliad*. The rout of the Latins and the subsequent confusion and terror at the gates are briefly reflected in Turnus's view of this event (*ut infractos adversos Marte Latinos, / defecisse videt*), but there is a time lapse, which could best be called vague, between the two books (*sua nunc promissa reposci, / se signari oculis*). The transition between the time when Turnus apparently feels forced to make good his promise to meet Aeneas in single combat (*ultro implacabilis ardet, / attollitque animos* [3–4]) and the time when he announces his decision to Latinus is supplied by the simile of the wounded, defiant lion (4–9); but where Turnus comes

from and where Turnus goes to meet Latinus are left to the readers'
imaginations (we may supply, I suppose, a room in the palace). It is
perhaps churlish to suggest that we must also imagine for ourselves the
entrances or presences of Amata and Lavinia; we must allow, to continue
the contrast with Homer, that in a sense Hecuba also arrives on the scene
out of thin air. Yet in Homer's shaping of the scene, once Priam is
clearly and naturally represented as standing anxiously on the ramparts,
responding to the commotion at the gates, it is hardly difficult to imag-
ine that Hecuba, also concerned by the sudden commotion and thereby
worried about Hector, is by his side. The appearance of Latinus has been
briefly (yet more or less adequately) prepared for by the sudden and
effective appearance (at court?) of Turnus:

> haud secus accenso gliscit violentia Turno:
> tum sic adfatur regem, atque ita turbidus infit.

> just so did violence
> urge on fanatic Turnus. Hectic, he
> cries out to King Latinus with these words.
>
> (12.9–10)

But Amata, whose presence and speech correspond to the presence and
speech of Hecuba in the Homeric model, bursts into the scene without
preparation; so, without preparation, the even more shadowy Lavinia
glides into it. The effect of these entrances or sudden presences suggests
less the theatrical (or dramatic) *appearance* that is typical of Homer than
the incantatory evocation of *personae* that one *hears,* say, in an ensemble
reading of *The Waste Land.* This is not to say, of course, that there is no
visual excellence in this scene; indeed, I shall soon argue that this par-
ticular scene shows a highly elaborate and highly effective visual orga-
nization. Rather, I am suggesting that the conventions of visualization
that are common in Homer are emphatically flouted by Virgil here, as
happens frequently.

Here, the clarity of picture that logical and sequential articulation
makes possible yields to a deliberate blurring. Virgil's queen has a form
and gestures as well as a voice and emotions and thoughts, but picture
and gesture—because of the lack of careful articulation and because of
stylization and compression of representation—do not mesh and are not
meant to mesh. Here, not only because of what Amata has to say but
also because of the manner in which Amata is rendered in her speaking,
we are reminded of Greek tragedy and, strangely enough, of Seneca.

When our attention becomes fixed on Amata, we become aware that we are now confronted with a distancing, a stylization, almost a contempt for verisimilitude that are utterly foreign to Homer but not at all alien to the stages of Athens or Milan. Hecuba may be larger than life, but, since she is Homer's creature, she is also full of life (the miracle of stylization *and,* almost, of naturalism that we witness in "and loosening her garment, with one hand she showed her breast" [22.80] defies imitation even as it defies analysis); Amata, on the other hand, cannot hide the fact that she is, whatever else she is, a mezzo-soprano: *flebat, et ardentem generum moritura tenebat* (55). "Virgil's besetting sin," wrote Housman to Mackail, "is the use of words too forcible for his thoughts, and the *moritura* of *Aeneid* 12.55 makes me blush for him whenever I think of it." It is not recorded, that I know of, whether Ribbeck blushed also; but he did the next best thing. He emended. *Monitura tenebat.* She becomes, that is, a sensible woman. She does not rush upon him, throw herself in his way as he attempts to stride from the room, catch him, and cling to him as if her life depended on him (as it does). Rather, having sage advice to give him, she takes him by the arm. No, the scene as Virgil imagines it, with the madness of Turnus expanding at each moment, demands precisely the extravagance, the histrionics, that *moritura* confers. Whether the word connotes only an adumbration of her resolve to die if Turnus dies—which she is to announce momentarily—or, with more excess, foreshadows her actual death (603), or represents a sudden deathly pallor, or suggests to us that we are supposed to feel the pathos of her situation (the word is used once again of Amata [602]; four times of Dido; once, brilliantly of Lausus [10.811]), it is unrealistic if what is wanted is a precise imitation of the emotions and state of mind of a woman in Amata's situation. Housman blushed, I presume, because his sensibility was embarrassed by what it took to be a failure of mimetic decorum. But Virgil is not trying to proffer intelligible realities; he is, through the eyes of Turnus, trying to imagine the incomprehensibility of reality by the disintegration of images. *Moritura,* then, is not Virgil's way of describing what Amata looked like or how she felt at this particular moment; it is rather a way of indicating a penumbra of doom that Turnus vaguely senses and that we observe—for us, a dreadful flash of clarity. An omniscient, an Homeric, narrator might very well have described Amata as being overcome by excitement or hysteria or anxiety. That he would have described her as *moritura* is doubtful. But the sinister, jarringly unrealistic prescience of the word, its emotional editorialization, is suitable to the frame of mind or of madness that Turnus is in, and for the purpose of suggesting how Turnus misperceives reality the word is as exact as its extravagance is troubling.

And so with *violaverit*. Perhaps, unwittingly, Housman blushed because he remembered Lavinia's blush, which is, of course, unforgettable. But why does she blush? What is it that her mother says that conjures up this manifestation of simple embarrassment or of delicate, shy, turbulent eroticism? *Ardentem generum / generum Aenean?* We know nothing whatever of Lavinia's conscious thoughts, much less of her private fantasies. Does she respond to the passion of Turnus? Has she toyed with notions of the glamorous Asiatic barbarian, a white sheik come to brighten her humdrum existence? One may speculate, but Virgil has seen to it that such speculation is as fruitless as it is boring. We are given nothing but a fleeting, tantalizing vision of possible erotic excitement, but that vision is as incisive and as artistic as anything Virgil wrote. Yet it was not imagined in order that we might understand something about Lavinia; it was imagined in order that we might understand something about Turnus. We do not know if Latinus or Amata notice their daughter's manifestation of shyness or involuntary revelation of hidden desires. But Turnus notices and he thinks he knows what her blush means. Sexual jealousy causes his own romantic notions to kindle higher, and his eroticism adds fuel to the martial fires that are already blazing out of control—the *violentia* of this scene can increase no more.

My point here is that we see Lavinia blush through Turnus's eyes, and it is Turnus's passion and his point of view that cause Virgil to select *violaverit* in order to render and to distort in the rendering the Homeric *miēnēi* of *Iliad* 4.141. What might otherwise seem, then, another flagrant example of gratuitous mannerism or slakeless *cacozelia* turns out to be determined by Virgil's careful shaping of Turnus's point of view. *Violaverit* echoes the *violentia* of Turnus that dominates this scene, as do *ardor, rubor, rubent, rubebit* (77), *ardentem generum*. But it is also a projection of Turnus's *violentia* onto Aeneas; it is also, possibly, a way of fantasizing punishment of Lavinia for her suspected impurity. It is erotic, sensuous, and violent, crystallizing the images of blood, anger, roses, the dawn of vengeance into a single, complex, ineffable feeling. The flawlessly mixed simile describes the confused manner in which Turnus sees Lavinia's blush, and the way he sees the blush and reacts to it describes the confusion that has now taken full possession of him as this final book opens and that will keep possession of him for the remainder of the poem.

Again, a contrast with Homer is in order. In its relation to Menelaus

(*Iliad* 4.141–47) the ivory dyed with crimson is emblematic both of the glory of his wound (*kosmos, kudos* [145]) and of his vitality and his health as warrior:

ὡς δ' ὅτε τίς τ' ἐλέφαντα γυνὴ φοίνικι μιήνῃ
Μηονὶς ἠὲ Κάειρα, παρήιον ἔμμεναι ἵππῳ·
κεῖται δ' ἐν θαλάμῳ, πολέες τέ μιν ἠρήσαντο
ἱππῆες φορέειν· βασιλῆι δὲ κεῖται ἄγαλμα,
ἀμφότερον κόσμος θ' ἵππῳ ἐλατῆρί τε κῦδος·
τοῖοί τοι, Μενέλαε, μιάνθην αἵματι μηροὶ
εὐφυέες κνῆμαί τε ἰδὲ σφυρὰ κάλ' ὑπένερθε.

When a woman from Maeonia or Caria stains with purple dye a piece of ivory that is destined for a bridle, it comes to be stored in the royal treasure and is coveted by many riders; but in the king's treasury it remains, at once an ornament for the horse and a special distinction for its rider. So, Menelaus, your thighs were stained blood-red, and your trim legs and your fine ankles.

(4.141–47)

Here the neat repetition, *mianthēn,* serves as an ironic foil to the brightness and health that are imagined in *euphuees* and *kala*: blood from the wound might be thought to defile Menelaus's health and beauty, but in fact it only accentuates them. In Virgil's simile, on the other hand, however lovely Lavinia's blush is, however much it betokens her delicacy, there is a suggestion of possible corruption; as her beauty is momentarily spoiled by her tears (*lacrimis . . . flagrantes perfusa genas*), as the lilies are at once denatured and perversely beautified by their mingling with the red roses, so, in the mind of Turnus, the beauty of Lavinia and her innocence are jeopardized by what appears to be her equivocal response to her mother's speech. Without *violaverit* the mixed similes would be perfectly unexceptionable; with it, they take on an elusive but ineradicable tinge of corruption; they are, with this single word, gathered into the confusion, frenzy, and suspicion that grip Turnus's mind and heart.

An essential aspect of Homer's narrative art is his ability to achieve inimitable unity from multiplicity. If we compare Virgil's scene with Homer's in respect of point of view, we discover that Homer, using an omniscient narrator, moving from the throng at the gates; to Apollo and Achilles; then to Hector, Priam, and Hecuba; and, finally, to Hector alone, has been able to bring Hector and the tragedy and inevitability of his death into a steady, unshakable focus. In Virgil, on the other hand, the epic narrator merges imperceptibly with Turnus himself; we begin and end the scene by viewing Turnus from outside, but in the center of the scene we hear and see the other characters for the most part as Turnus hears and sees them, and, as a result of this shifting of focus and this absence of narrative distancing, we find ourselves in the situation that confronted us in book 4 with Dido: because we are, in some ways, too close to the narrator-protagonist, we are often unable to distinguish between what is taking place and what the hypersensitive narrator-protagonist believes is taking place, and we are at last unable to extricate ourselves from the illusions of a character whose words and actions we are supposed to be evaluating at some degree of distance. In the case of Turnus, as in the case of Dido, we are necessarily by turns critical and sympathetic, yet we have finally no absolute index which enables us to distinguish truth from illusion; even though we understand that their perceptions are to some extent deranged, we do not know, cannot know, to what extent they are deranged, and, in any case, we must frequently depend on the information they offer us because no other information is available. In the case of Turnus, the shifting of narrative focus, the fluctuation of rhetorical emphasis, the hyperbole that is indicative of distortions that cannot quite be corrected, result in a baffling, disquieting uncertainty about who Turnus is, what he is doing, what is destroying him. This is not to suggest that Turnus is a complicated character and Hector a simple one. Hector shows pride, vanity, heroism, sense of responsibility and love, even as Turnus does, but in the scene in question the proof of Hector's final integrity is the desperate soliloquy in which he confronts and (unconsciously) masters his own uncertainties about himself. The measure of Turnus's final confusion about his motives and himself is the bluster and ranting that mark this scene's close. The crazed arrogance of Turnus's final speech in this scene compares unfavorably both with the vitality and candor of his speech against Drances in book 11 and with Hector's self-scrutiny and essential humility in the soliloquy of book 22. The vestiges of Turnus's earlier heroism dissolve before our eyes into the deceptive, destructive sweetness of the mixed similes. Soldier's honor, gallant patriotism, lover's passion are separated from one another at the very moment they ought to be united. Whereas Hector pulls himself together, is pulled together by the momentum of Homer's narrative, in Virgil's narrative Turnus in this scene is unmanned, and his image disintegrates under the pressure of the *violentia* which is reflected in oxymoron, hyperbole, blurred simile, and shifting point of view. A deliberately violent and disordered poetics faithfully records a turbulent unintelligibility; this deliberate failure of images is a way of showing darkness.

II. Dissolving Pathos

volvitur Euryalus leto, pulchrosque per artus
it cruor; inque umeros cervix collapsa recumbit:
purpureus veluti cum flos succisus aratro
languescit moriens, lassove papavera collo
demisere caput, pluvia cum forte gravantur.

He tumbles into death, the blood flows down
his handsome limbs; his neck, collapsing, leans
against his shoulder: even as a purple
flower, severed by the plow, falls slack in death;
or poppies as, with weary necks, they bow
their heads when weighted down by sudden rain.

(9.433–37)

ἦ ῥα, καὶ ἄλλον ὀϊστὸν ἀπὸ νευρῆφιν ἴαλλεν
Ἕκτορος ἀντικρύ, βαλέειν δέ ἑ ἵετο θυμός.
καὶ τοῦ μέν ῥ' ἀφάμαρθ', ὁ δ' ἀμύμονα Γοργυθίωνα,
υἱὸν ἐῢν Πριάμοιο, κατὰ στῆθος βάλεν ἰῷ
τόν ῥ' ἐξ Αἰσύμηθεν ὀπυιομένη τέκε μήτηρ,
καλὴ Καστιάνειρα, δέμας σεικυῖα θεῆσι.
μήκων δ' ὡς ἑτέρωσε κάρη βάλεν, ἥ τ' ἐνὶ κήπῳ,
καρπῷ βριθομένη νοτίῃσί τε σειαρινῇσιν·
ὣς ἑτέρωσ' ἤμυσε κάρη πήληκι βαρυνθέν.

He spoke and from his bowstring shot another arrow direct at Hector, and his heart yearned to wound him. Hector he missed, but Gorgythion, the fine son of Priam, his arrow struck, the chest pierced. Him Castianeira bore, Priam's wife, a woman from Aisyme—the beautiful Castianeira, like a goddess in form and figure. As a poppy in a garden lolls its head to one side, heavy with seed and spring rain, so, weighted with its casque, to one side dangled his head.

(Iliad 8.300–308)

δούπησεν δὲ πεσών, ἀράβησε δὲ τεύχε' ἐπ' αὐτῷ.
αἵματί οἱ δεύοντο κόμαι Χαρίτεσσιν ὁμοῖαι

πλοχμοί θ', οἳ χρυσῷ τε καὶ ἀργύρῳ ἐσφήκωντο.
οἷον δὲ τρέφει ἔρνος ἀνὴρ ἐριθηλὲς ἐλαίης
χώρῳ ἐν οἰοπόλῳ, ὅθ' ἅλις ἀναβέβροχεν ὕδωρ,
καλὸν τηλεθάον· τὸ δέ τε πνοιαὶ δονέουσι
παντοίων ἀνέμων, καί τε βρύει ἄνθεϊ λευκῷ·
ἐλθὼν δ' ἐξαπίνης ἄνεμος σὺν λαίλαπι πολλῇ
βόθρου τ' ἐξέστρεψε καὶ ἐξετάνυσσ' ἐπὶ γαίη·
τοῖον Πανθόου υἱὸν ἐϋμμελίην Εὔφορβον
Ἀτρεΐδης Μενέλαος ἐπεὶ κτάνε, τεύχε' ἐσύλα.

And he fell with a dull clang, and his armor rattled about him as he fell, and his hair, lovely as the hair of the Graces themselves, and his braids, clasped with gold and silver, were soaked with his blood. And like a flourishing young olive tree that someone tends in a quiet place where fertile water gushes, a tree that flowers, flowers in beauty, and it is shaken by every windy current, and it thrives in the whitenss of its blossoms— then a sudden wind with great whirling beats down and up-roots it from its trench, flings it on the ground: even so was Euphorbus of the stout ashen spear, he, the son of Panthous, whom Menelaus, son of Atreus, killed and fell to despoiling.

(*Iliad* 17.50–60)

nec meum respectet, ut ante, amorem,
qui illius culpa cecidit velut prati
ultimi flos, praetereunte postquam
tactus aratro est.

nor let her regard, as she did before, my love—
the love of him who, because of her sin, has fallen,
like a blossom at the field's edge, when the passing
plough has grazed it.

(Catullus 11)

This grouping of passages suggests two things that we will want to keep in mind about the Virgilian simile in question: (1) for all the sim-plicity of its syntax and for all the brevity and clarity of its imagery, it is, *because* of its extreme compression, a highly elaborate and carefully organized *literary* contrivance that is as conspicuously artificial in its methods as it is in its ends; (2) Homer understood the artistic possibilities of pathos fully, but, because the essential nature of his art is tragic, he uses pathos sparingly, chiefly for purposes of ornament and relief. Virgil, whose art is essentially lyrical, uses pathos frequently, as is commonly known: it is the reason for, and the nature of, Virgilian pathos that I am trying to approach in this section of my examination of his poetics.

Two aspects of the Virgilian passage seem to me specially remarkable. First, the death of Euryalus is possessed of an extraordinary loveliness that is wholly appropriate to the tone and function of the Virgilian *Doloneia,* yet the beauty of these verses calls attention to itself in a way that impedes the progress of the narrative. In a certain way, they are too beautiful even for the climax of the dreamlike adventures of Euryalus and Nisus; they want almost to be excerpted from their surroundings, to be pondered over, repeated. Second, beneath their loveliness, the verses exhibit something that smacks of the grotesque, of *Liebestod.* Though Virgil is careful to understate the eroticism of the entire passage, he gives it vivid emphasis at the climax of this narrative: the physical beauty of Euryalus and a sudden vision of his unheroic fragility and helplessness are so stressed as to give emotional significance to the final act of the dying Nisus:

> tum super exanimum sese proiecit amicum
> confossus, placidaque ibi demum morte quievit.

> Then, pierced, he cast himself upon his lifeless
> friend; there, at last, he found his rest in death.
> (9.444–45)

The death of Nisus, in its grim violence (*exanimum amicum / proiecit / confossus*) and in its gentleness (*placida morte / quievit*), shows a sort of oxymoronic juxtaposition of opposites not dissimilar to the fused discrepancies of the Euryalus simile. The death of Euryalus is depicted as being pretty, not particularly noble; the death of Nisus, dissolving as it does into the previous images of blood and of blossoms broken and weary, attains a pose of nobility both by reason of his gesture of love and devotion and by reason of Virgil's patriotic apostrophe to the reckless, vainglorious lovers:

> fortunati ambo! si quid mea carmina possunt,
> nulla dies umquam memori vos eximet aevo.

> Fortunate pair! If there be any power
> within my poetry, no day shall ever
> erase you from the memory of time.
> (9.446–47)

The story may affect us in several ways: We may feel sympathy for the young men, and we may admire their courage and reciprocal devotion, even though we cannot admire their intelligence; at another level we may feel that the Nisus-Euryalus episode functions chiefly as retardation of the central action (the arming of Aeneas) and as preparation for the *aristeia* of Turnus, which fills the rest of book 9; or we may decide that Nisus and Euryalus have been deliberately sentimentalized and that the *Doloneia* has been carefully travestied in order to stress the nature of vainglory and to challenge the foundations of the epic sensibility. We may react in one or in all of these ways at different times, but one thing about the close of the narrative remains constant: the death of Euryalus—and, by extension, the death of Nisus—signals a retreat from Homeric mimesis by its mannered conflation of Homeric imagery and Catullan imagery, and it annihilates the possibility of our finding in these deaths a tragic statement about the necessity that governs human existence; we cannot say of these deaths, as we can say of so many deaths in the *Iliad*: "it was an actuality—stern, mournful, and fine." Not because Virgil did not understand such actuality, not because Virgil did not understand what Homer had imagined; rather, because in the universe that Virgil imagines the knowledge that would make such an actuality intelligible is not available and because, therefore, such actualities are literally intolerable and are therefore minimized in a variety of ways. In a sense, the dissolving pathos of Virgil may seem a coward's stratagem to shield him and us from truths we cannot endure to see; in a deeper sense, the dissolving pathos functions ironically—it stresses both the immensity of what confronts human existence and our utter nakedness before that immensity. But to test these descriptions of Virgilian pathos, we must now turn to the Homeric originals that they at once imitate and transform.

The death of Gorgythion is the stuff pathos is made of, for he receives the arrow that Teucer had intended for Hector; so, at *Aeneid* 10.781ff., the pathos of accidental death is represented in this fashion:

> sternitur infelix alieno vulnere, caelumque
> aspicit, et dulces moriens reminiscitur Argos.

> Luckless, he has been laid low by a wound
> not meant for him; he looks up at the sky
> and, dying, calls to mind his gentle Argos.
> (10.781–82)

Gorgythion, then, dies *alieno vulnere*. But where Virgil offers a compressed, almost dry catachresis to evoke a misfortune that would otherwise beggar language, Homer characteristically uses delicate and reserved modulation:

> Hector he missed, but Gorgythion, the fine son of Priam, his arrow struck, the chest pierced. Him Castianeira bore, Priam's wife, a woman from Aisyme—the beautiful Castianeira, like a goddess in form and figure.
>
> (8.302–5)

Teucer missed Hector and hit Gorgythion, who is *amumōn*, the son of Priam and Castianeria, *kalē, demas eikuia theēisi*. The familiar, limpid epithets are at once soothing and inevitable. The young man's death is an unfortunate accident, and he himself is almost incidental; he has strayed into the story and he strays out of it, a ripple on the bright violent stream. The pathos of his dying is restrained and tactful: his youth and vulnerability, the fact that he is, in a sense, merely a bystander, a victim of an inexplicable process that is beyond Homer's comprehension and ours—these things are balanced by his vigor and manliness. The poppy is beaten down by spring rains, but this possible suggestion of weakness is offset by *karpōi brithomenē*; Gorgythion is undone by circumstances, but he is healthy; indeed, it is his flourishing, his ripeness that have exposed him to the common hazards of existence and the special hazards of warfare that are symbolized by the rains. Furthermore, his head is bowed in death by the weight of his helmet: he dies a soldier's death, and the imagery that depicts that death is a handsome fusion of his vulnerability and his strength. In this sense, the pathos of the simile is subsumed, as is customary in the *Iliad,* into a larger vision of the nature of things. A wavering sense of inexplicable disaster, then grace and tenderness, then a brief sorrow, then the inevitable, *es muss sein.* He is young and full of life, yes. But he is also a soldier, he has accepted this role; such things happen to soldiers, he must accept this, does accept it, and so must we. I have belabored what Homer consummately understates in order to show that Homer uses pathos to transcend what would else be merely pitiful and thereby to attain, here as elsewhere, that strange tragic sense that is at once utterly ideal and utterly real. The pathos serves only to lead us beyond pathos to a sober, strangely comforting truth.

Compared with the dead Gorgythion (and it is well to bear in mind that Virgil not only invites but demands the comparison), Euryalus seems like a ruined mannequin. Where Homer had allowed us only to guess at Gorgythion's looks from his descriptions of Castianeira and from the indirect and terse imagery that evokes the poppy, Virgil emphatically asserts the beauty of Euryalus (*pulchros per artus*) and elaborates on it further by his handling of *purpureus flos* and *papavera*. This beauty is not merely vulnerable, it is utterly defenseless, and its pitiful demise is unrelieved by wider perspectives: we are locked into a sweet, tainted melancholy that the patriotic apostrophe, so far from exorcizing, can only foil with ironic indecorum. The echo of Catullus's self-mocking, pathetic lover, a dear little flower mangled by Vagina Dentata, merges (or, rather, fails to merge) with the echo of Homer's unfortunate young warrior. *Pēlēki barunthen* nudges us away from this mood back into the story. *Languescit moriens* and *lasso collo* create a stifling, mesmerizing stasis; their sentimentality side-steps the fact of disaster so that what is fearful about this death lingers—beautified, unresolved, and corrupt.

Lest it be thought that this comparison, though chosen by Virgil himself, is unfair because Gorgythion is a walk-on, let us glance briefly at the death simile of Euphorbus, a figure whom Homer develops at some length. Euphorbus, a not unlikable and a recognizable blend of audacity, swagger, vanity, and prudence, incapacitates Patroclus with a cast of his spear, thus putting the finishing touches to Apollo's work and getting him ready for Hector; after wounding his man, he ducks back in the crowd, emerging to look to his spoils only after Hector has killed Patroclus; then follows a shouting match with Menelaus, after which Menelaus kills him (*Iliad* 16.806–15; 17.1ff.). It would be too much to say that, in this poem at least, Euphorbus's death is a matter of poetic justice; it is rather the natural outcome of who the man is and what he does and wants. He is vain about the luxuriance of his hair, a fact that amuses Homer and that he uses with delicate irony: the hair that reminded one of the Graces (reminded Euphorbus of the Graces, too) was once set off with gold and silver and is now adorned with his blood. It is a fact, not a judgment; it is noted down and let go. Otherwise he is a remarkably accomplished warrior for so young a man (16.808–11); he naturally challenges Menelaus and he naturally pays for it. Euphorbus is not an incidental character and his death is not accidental, but Homer touches it with a light pathos. The luxuriant hair and the ordinary youthful bluster are illumined by the splendid image of the olive tree, grown to near maturity, its white blossoms shaken by every wind (*pnoiai pantoiōn anemōn*), then suddenly set upon by a wind whose terrific force (*anemos sun lailapi pollēi*) it cannot withstand, by which it is uprooted and toppled to the ground. Sad? Yes. Intolerable? No. The zest and vigor are as admirable as the self-confidence and the naïveté are touching, but the nature of things is unalterable. With Euphorbus as with Gorgythion, it is the pathos itself that disappears, dissolved into a clarity that has no time for prolonged grief that may grow to unappeasable melancholy: *Atreidēs Menelaos epei ktane, teuche' esula.* The gaze is steady, but not dispassionate; the eyes pity but do not succumb to despair or terror. This is a far cry from the melting, languid rhythms and the soft equivocal images that Virgil uses to prevent us from seeing the death of Euryalus as it is. We can grieve for both Gorgythion and for Euphorbus because we can admire them and, in large measure, understand them; we admire and in part understand them because we see them through the eyes of a tactful, helpful, and unobtrusive narrator who constantly persuades us that he is as omniscient and as trustworthy as is necessary for our purposes and his. We feel sorry for Euryalus, but that pity yields to an insoluble mysterious anxiety; we forget exactly who the beautiful lover was. His lover embraces him in death and they are joined forever. The glamorous broken doll and his lover are eternal patriots of Rome? What have their deaths, their romance, their mindless, murderous rampage to do with the destiny of Rome? We never find out. We see the death of Euryalus through the eyes of a narrator whose vision is colored by the terror and passion of Nisus. When Nisus dies, the picture disintegrates before our eyes. If what we feel as a result of that disintegration is "doubt and carnal fear," that is what Virgil wants us to feel.

> tum Iuno omnipotens, longum miserata dolorem
> difficilesque obitus, Irim demisit Olympo,
> quae luctantem animam nexosque resolveret artus.
> nam, quia nec fato merita nec morte peribat,
> sed misera ante diem, subitoque accensa furore,
> necdum illi flavum Proserpina vertice crinem
> abstulerat, Stygioque caput damnaverat Orco.
> ergo Iris croceis per caelum roscida pennis,
> mille trahens varios adverso sole colores,
> devolat, et supra caput adstitit: "hunc ego Diti
> sacrum iussa fero, teque isto corpore solvo."
> sic ait, et dextra crinem secat. omnis et una
> dilapsus calor, atque in ventos vita recessit.

But then all-able Juno pitied her
long sorrow and hard death and from Olympus
sent Iris down to free the struggling spirit
from her entwining limbs. For as she died
a death that was not merited or fated,
but miserable and before her time
and spurred by sudden frenzy, Proserpina
had not yet cut a gold lock from her crown,
not yet assigned her life to Stygian Orcus.
On saffron wings dew-glittering Iris glides
along the sky, drawing a thousand shifting
colors across the facing sun. She halted
above the head of Dido: "So commanded,
I take this lock as offering to Dis;
I free you from your body." So she speaks
and cuts the lock with her right hand; at once
the warmth was gone, the life passed to the winds.

(4.693–705)

In dealing with these verses, our special concern will be to examine the way in which Iris's epiphany, the shifting beauty of the rainbow that betokens her coming, distracts our attention from the fact of Dido's suffering and thereby blurs the significance of that suffering. But before we turn to this characteristic Virgilian *Kunstbegriff,* the scumbling of his outlines, we had best examine the question of point of view in this passage. At first glance one might suppose that we have only to do with an ordinary narrator who is reporting this event as he sees it. If we look more closely, however, and remember that, for the most part, the events of book 4 unfold before us as Dido experiences them, we are confronted with several hard complexities. Is Dido aware that Iris has come? Does she hear the words that we hear? Is it possible that Dido sees the rainbow that we see and hears the death formula as we hear it? We know, at least, that the last time we see her clearly (*ter revoluta toro est, oculisque errantibus alto / quaesivit caelo lucem, ingemuitque reperta* [691–92]), her eyes are fixed on the light of the sky. *Ingemuitque reperta,* not admired by Racine alone, is justly celebrated, but it is so flawless as to defy translation, or paraphrase, or explanation. *Ingemuit* is, poetically speaking, *sui causa*—a perfectly accurate and perfectly simple metaphor for dying, looking one's last on the light of day. Yet she does not, or does not seem to, die at this moment. She dies when Iris, having descended in glory, has spoken the death formula and snipped off the gold lock of hair. My suggestion here is that the two moments that appear to be separated (*ingemuit, vita recessit*) are all but simultaneous: in short, we see Dido's death as Dido "sees" it, the fatal ritual utterance of Iris, the death blow (*crinem secat*), the groan. What Dido finds (*reperta*) as she anxiously searches the sky is the doom and the deliverance that Iris brings: the light is the shining fatal appearance of Juno's messenger. This baffling (and artistic) division of one instant into what seems to be two instants—indeed, into a succession of events—has the curious effect of removing us from Dido even while we remain with her. The division is accomplished by the unobtrusive intrusion of a voice that is, properly speaking, alien to what seems to be the tone and the function of this scene. *Tum Iuno omnipotens, longum miserata dolorem.* On one level, this verse and those that directly follow it are spoken by the ordinary narrator, who is explaining what Juno does when she views Dido's agony and why she does it. But this level, which is one of direct, sequential narration, is rather deceptive here, as elsewhere in the poem. Is the regular narrator calling Juno *omnipotens*? If so, why? He must surely know that much of his poem is directed to showing that *omnipotens* is one thing that she is precisely not. Is it careless cliché that is essentially occasioned by metrical necessities or vague intuitions of oral composition? Not, probably, in this poem. Is it ironic? Perhaps, but if Virgil is merely being ironic, on this level, at Juno's expense (or Dido's), the irony is tasteless and cheap. And what of *miserata*? Juno's compassion is reminiscent of the compassion shown by Ovid's deities: it is utterly out of character, and, if we consider Juno's role in what has happened to Dido, a hypocritical, disgusting turn of the screw. The abruptness of Juno's appearance at this point in the narrative is as distracting from the business at hand as her omnipotence and her compassion. For a moment, our attention is focused on Juno and what she thinks she ought to feel about the event that is taking place; this focus prepares us for the brilliance of Iris's descent, which engages our attention for the rest of the close of book 4, until the last sentence, when we return to the event proper. And this means that our attention has been averted from what is of central importance about Dido's death to peripheral details about the death; and in this process the gravity and the significance of Dido's death are lost from view. From *tum Iuno omnipotens* down to *damnaverat Orco* we have entered into the mind of Juno. It is she who describes herself as *omnipotens,* and it is she who describes herself as *miserata* and then goes on to give a clear and accurate account of Dido's tragedy and her innocence (*nam, quia nec fato*). Readers who persist in thinking Dido guilty of wrongdoing have at least the excuse that the only clear vindication of her behavior is put in the mind of a character whom we know we cannot trust. Our natural distrust of Juno, coupled as it is here with the casual appearance of *omnipotens* and *miserata*, creates a bewildering admixture of illusion and truth and acts as a proper transition to the dazzling imagery that marks the epiphany of Iris, the death of Dido, and the finale of book 4.

The use of color in the entire passage is at once notable and characteristic. The tawny gold of Dido's hair is foiled by gruesome darkness (*Stygio Orco*), then radiant yellows and fresh translucency (*croceis pennis, roscida*), and, finally, the splendid swirling indistinction of *mille trahens varios adverso sole colores. Varius . . .* is a favorite word with Virgil when he wishes to stress complexity and confusion. Here the word paradoxically at once presents a vision and annihilates that vision with excessive brightness. Hence, a delusive splendor throws a beautiful yet sinister screen between us and what we assumed we were meant to see. For us, as for Dido, it is precisely the moment when the light is at its fullest that the apprehension of darkness overtakes us. What was supposed to illuminate Dido's death obscures its significance in a frustrating, almost sinister way. Before the intrusion of Juno and Iris, Dido's imminent death—though painful and terrible—was affecting and not without its own courage and nobility. But with the appearance of Iris, Dido's autonomy fails; her death is gathered into a beauty that, colored as it is by *miserata* and *misera,* is almost sentimental; and yet, juxtaposed with that beauty—indeed, heightened by it—are the remorseless grimly supernatural words of Iris: *hunc ego Diti / sacrum iussa fero, teque isto corpore solvo.* The effect of the brilliant imagery and the cold laconic speech differs considerably from the effect that Homer achieves in a passage where Athena descends at Zeus's behest to spur the Greeks on to get possession of Patroclus's body:

> ἠΰτε πορφυρέην ἶριν θνητοῖσι τανύσσῃ
> Ζεὺς ἐξ οὐρανόθεν, τέρας ἔμμεναι ἢ πολέμοιο
> ἢ καὶ χειμῶνος δυσθαλπέος, ὅς ῥά τε ἔργων
> ἀνθρώπους ἀνέπαυσεν ἐπὶ χθονί, μῆλα δὲ κήδει,
> ὣς ἡ πορφυρέη νεφέλη πυκάσασα ἓ αὐτὴν
> δύσετ᾽ Ἀχαιῶν ἔθνος, ἔγειρε δὲ φῶτα ἕκαστον.

When Zeus from the heavens unrolls the rainbow that glints darkling to be a signal of war or of uncomfortable winter, he

forces mortal men to cease from their labors on the earth,
and he troubles their flocks—even so, Athena, swathing her-
self in a darkly glinting cloud, entered into the crowds of
Achaeans and goaded on each man.

(17.547–52)

Here the color word, *porphuros,* reverberates with a sinister, inhuman
foreboding, but for all its menace, the word and the imagery that attends
upon it nevertheless denote realistically a disruption of the *natural* order
(*teras-wergōn anthropōus anepausen, mēla de kēdei*). Furthermore, the color
word is not used here, as the words of Virgil are used, to paint a pretty
picture: the word is, beyond its realism, ominous, and its central function
is to represent the superhumanity of Athena in her unpersuadable pur-
pose. In Virgil the sweetness and light enchant and distract us at a
moment of hazard; then, through conflicting dread and sensuous delight,
we are propelled into a disintegration and a void where there is room
for neither pleasure nor the original seriousness: *omnis et una / dilapsus
calor, atque in ventos vita recessit.*

In this passage, then, the blurred imagery and wavering narrative
focus combine to create an unexpected and, in respect to tragic canons,
somewhat inappropriate pathos that first obscures and then nullifies the
nature and the significance of Dido's death. Since we see her in book 4
primarily through her own eyes, her courage, her magnanimity, and her
honesty (*et nunc magna mei sub terras ibit imago*) are seen fitfully and are
increasingly gathered into the confusions and misperceptions of her fren-
zies and agony. And if some of her essential nobility begins to be manifest
itself in her death throes (*illa, graves oculos conata attollere, rursus / deficit*),
that impulse to tragic sublimity and to dignity of death is immediately
submerged in the petty hyprocisies of Juno and the beautified terror of
the very close. Once again, a comparison with Homer may help us to
focus on the quality of the Virgilian pathos. Just as Sarpedon is about
to be killed by Patroclus, Zeus cries to Hera that he feels torn by con-
flicting desires (*dichtha de moi kradiē memone phresin hormainonti,* The heart
in my breast is balanced between two ways as I ponder [16.435]) in his
pity (*eleēse* [431]) for his son: he wants to submit to Fate, but he wants
even more to save Sarpedon. Hera points out that it would be unwise
of Zeus to do this, since other gods, who have loved ones among the
mortals, would certainly want to imitate his action. Then she (and Ho-
mer) mitigates the full anguish of Sarpedon's death with some of the
gentlest and most beautiful lines in the *Iliad*:

ἀλλ’ εἴ τοι φίλος ἐστί, τεὸν δ’ ὀλοφύρεται ἦτορ,
ἤ τοι μέν μιν ἔασον ἐνὶ κρατερῇ ὑσμίνῃ
χέρσ’ ὕπο Πατρόκλοιο Μενοιτιάδαο δαμῆναι·
αὐτὰρ ἐπεὶ δὴ τόν γε λίπῃ ψυχή τε καὶ αἰών,
πέμπειν μιν Θάνατόν τε φέρειν καὶ νήδυμον Ὕπνον,
εἰς ὅ κε δὴ Λυκίης εὐρείης δῆμον ἵκωνται,
ἔνθα ἑ ταρχύσουσι κασίγνητοί τε ἔται τε
τύμβῳ τε στήλῃ τε· τὸ γὰρ γέρας ἐστὶ θανόντων.

But if he is dear to you and if your heart is grieved for him,
nevertheless let him be mastered by the hands of Patroclus,
son of Menoetius, in harsh encounter; but when his soul and
his lifetime have abandoned him, charge Death and kind Sleep
to bear him off until they come to the land of wide Lycia
where his brothers and his friends will bury him with tomb
and monument. For such is the recompense of the dead.

(*Iliad* 16.450–57)

The juxtaposition of death and sleep borders on oxymoron, for though
sleep is in a sense like death, sleep entails life and is thus the opposite
of death; there is, then, a *coincidentia oppositorum,* a new unity that tran-
scends mere euphemism and modulates softly into the simple splendor
of *to gar geras esti thanontōn.* This blending of gentle solace and martial
glory is enough:

ὣς ἔφατ’, οὐδ’ ἀπίθησε πατὴρ ἀνδρῶν τε θεῶν τε.
αἱματοέσσας δὲ ψιάδας κατέχευεν ἔραζε
παῖδα φίλον τιμῶν, τόν οἱ Πάτροκλος ἔμελλε
φθίσειν ἐν Τροῖῃ ἐριβώλακι, τηλόθι πάτρης.

Thus she spoke, and the father of men and gods was not
unpersuaded by her words. And tears of blood he wept upon
the earth, his dear son thus honoring—Sarpedon, whom Pa-
troclus was about to destroy, there on the fertile soil of Troy,
far away from his own country.

(16.458–61)

Zeus is persuaded and composed, the grief is pondered and let go of.
Then the inexorable movement to disaster begins again, and Sarpedon
dies with the magnificent ease and courage that befit a son of Zeus. It
is a spare pathos, enough to light up the depth of feeling and the good
sense of Zeus, enough to foil the heroism of Sarpedon, not enough to

ruin the bright firm outlines of their dignity. In a way that we might be tempted to describe as Stoic, feelings are allowed to function in their natural way, but they are not allowed to overwhelm the characters or the audience and thereby to deprive them of their ability to understand what they are doing and what is happening.

In the Virgilian passage what first appears to be gentleness is not balanced by anything, and the beauty gradually overwhelms and dissolves the dignity of Dido's death and with it the meaning of her life and the authenticity of her struggles. This sleight of hand is accomplished with a very few words, which are carefully set in a deceptively short and simple description of Dido's final moments: *omnipotens, miserata, misera, nec merita morte, croceis, pennis, roscida, mille varios colores trahens.* In the beauty of the picture and in the heartsick loveliness of the cadences, we may no longer remember that this frustrated and agonized woman is, by the testimony of the goddess herself, essentially the victim of the deity who proffers her a release from her torment. For this reason, there is a strangely disturbing fraudulence about this gentle demise. Part of this fraudulence is achieved by means of the ironic manipulations of pathos; part of it is achieved by a deliberate confusion of narrators: the view of Dido is superimposed on the view of the epic narrator, and on this delicate complexity there is further superimposed the view of Juno. In this composite image, the outlines of the final scene—and indeed of book 4 as a whole—are blurred, and the action of this book and the significance of its leading character find no still center; the story of Dido drifts away from us, its momentum and conflicts are not gathered into a vanishing point, so they move off into book 6 and beyond it to book 12, nor do they find unity or perspective anyplace in the poem.

> at vero ut vultum vidit morientis et ora,
> ora modis Anchisiades pallentia miris,
> ingemuit miserans graviter dextramque tetendit,
> et mentem patriae subiit pietatis imago.

> But when he saw the look and face of dying
> Lausus—he was mysteriously pale—
> Anchises' son sighed heavily with pity
> and stretched out his right hand; the image of
> his love for his own father touched his mind.
>   (10.821–24)

These verses show a remarkable blending of simplicity of phrasing and syntax with rich elaborations and compressions of emotion. The first, third, and fourth verses are beautifully offset in their clarity and vigor by the aureate impressionism of the second verse, where the repetition of *ora,* the alternation of dactyls and spondees, and the patronymic, framed by caesuras, combine to fashion an unearthly, almost dreamlike languor. This quality of unreality is further augmented by Virgil's stress on Aeneas's intellectual response, apart from his compassion, to the death of Lausus: the young man's death becomes a kind of symbol or paradigm of filial devotion (*patriae pietatis imago*) that transcends this specific death. It is towards this paradigm of the virtue that Aeneas holds most dear that he responds with such emotion, and it is to this virtue that Aeneas addresses his great speech. The confrontation in this scene, then, is between Aeneas and himself, for, though the scene may in part remind us of the scene between Achilles and Lycaon in *Iliad* 21, there is no actual dramatic confrontation between Aeneas and Lausus. Lausus is dead when Aeneas speaks to him in a truly personal way; the initial cry, *quo moriture, ruis, maioraque viribus audes? / fallit te incautum pietas tua,* in its bitter irony, prepares us for the speech that follows, but it evokes no response from Lausus, and, characteristically, Virgil does not, in the Homeric manner, offer a dialogue wherein the opposing characters verbalize their conflicts as well as enact them. The conflict here, as in the scenes with Dido and the final scene with Turnus, is between the piety that is defined by patriotism and the larger, almost Epicurean piety that feels not only responsibility for persons of one's own family and *civitas* but also for persons whose humanity and suffering demand one's respect and help. In the dead Lausus Aeneas recognizes, unconsciously, himself, or rather, the part of himself that he most respects, that is most essentially his true self. And in his killing of this image of himself, Aeneas adumbrates the final scene of the poem where, in killing Turnus, he is forced to abandon compassion because he is finally caught in the fine web of *ira* and of patriotic obligations that are, in respect of the ideal compassion, rather narrow. The scene, then, is emblematic of one of the great themes of the poem, *Anchisiades:* we remember the great scene between Priam and Neoptolemus in book 2, and, more important, we remember the superlative moment between Achilles and Priam in *Iliad* 24:

> ὣς φάτο, τῷ δ' ἄρα πατρὸς ὑφ' ἵμερον ὦρσε γόοιο·
> ἁψάμενος δ' ἄρα χειρὸς ἀπώσατο ἦκα γέροντα.
> τὼ δὲ μνησαμένω, ὁ μὲν Ἕκτορος ἀνδροφόνοιο

κλαῖ' ἀδινά, προπάροιθε ποδῶν Ἀχιλῆος ἐλυσθείς,
αὐτὰρ Ἀχιλλεὺς κλαῖεν ἑὸν πατέρ', ἄλλοτε δ' αὖτε
Πάτροκλον· τῶν δὲ στοναχὴ κατὰ δώματ' ὀρώρει.

Thus Priam spoke and set Achilles craving to lament his own
father. And Achilles clasped the old man's hand and gently he
pushed him from him. So the two men pondered their dead
in memory: Priam, hunched at the feet of Achilles, wept
helplessly for Hector, killer of men, and Achilles now wept
for his father, now for Patroclus. And the noise of their an-
guish streamed throughout the dwelling.

(*Iliad* 24.507–12)

Here, for a brief inimitable moment, pitiless anger and bitterness are
relived by common grief. The impossibility of true reconciliation be-
tween these two will flare up again very soon (552–70) when Priam
overplays his hand, but, if it is wishful thinking, indeed, misguided
sentimentality, to speak of character change in Achilles, here or any-
where, we must nevertheless acknowledge that Achilles' sympathy for
Priam and his willingness to suspend his bitterness temporarily shadow
forth a profound and authentic humanity. But this vision of common
suffering as compassion arises naturally out of the character of Achilles
and the situation in which he finds himself. The compassion of Aeneas,
though it is not—like the compassion of Juno in the previous passage—
so inexplicable as to seem hypocritical, though it is utterly in character,
takes us by surprise, for the epic battlefield is not the place for this kind
of compassion. This seeming indecorum reminds us that, in a very real
sense, the epic battlefield is not the place for Aeneas, that the hero of
this poem is constantly forced to act against his instincts and his most
cherished beliefs and ideals in a way that would be unthinkable for an
Iliadic hero. This is not to say that Achilles is a pitiless monster. In *alla,
philos, thane kai su* (*Iliad* 21.106ff.) we glimpse beneath the cruel irony a
stern pity that, as in the scene with Priam, issues from a restrained yet
flawless intuition of universal suffering and common doom: *all' epi toi
kai emoi thanatos kai moira krataiē* [Yet even I have also my death and my
strong destiny] (21.110).

In this passage of Virgil such an exact and ruthless closing with
tragic vision is not to be found. Virgil has discovered here the heart of
his poem, the greatness of the human spirit (as it is reflected in *pietas*)
ruined by murderous unreason (*violentia, ira*), but the fullness of this
terrifying vision is shadowed with pathos and sentiment and is further

obscured by Aeneas's own delusions: he still imagines that it will be possible for him to perform the role that destiny has thrust on him and to preserve the integrity of his personal sensitivity and decency. But, again, the Epicurean saint has no place on the field of carnage, and there is something particularly horrifying in the Epicurean expressing this kind of sentiment just after he has killed his man. The final emphasis on this conflict and on the moral dangers of *pietas* Virgil properly reserves for the end of the poem. Here that ruin is adumbrated by Aeneas's unconscious recognition of the fact that he cannot quite be both the patriot and the sage. His compassion for the dead Lausus is itself pathetic because it is futile and reflects the hazard to his ideas. Yet the fact of this futility is too dark, too harsh, too intolerable. So, as is frequently the case, it is rendered opaquely. With the words *moriture* (811), *tunicam, molli mater quam neverat auro* (818), *ingemuit miserans* (823), *miserande puer* (825), and *ipsum / sanguine turpantem comptos de more capillos* (831–32) we find ourselves once again screened, by a delicate haze, a melancholy loveliness, from realities that are unbearable in exact proportion as they are unintelligible. But these stratagems of solace are deliberately deceptive. In Virgil, the darkness does not serve to foil the light; rather, the light illumines the quality and the extent of darkness. And as the brightness of Virgil's images tends to dissolve so as to reveal an essential night, so his tenderness and wistful regard illumine a universe in which such feelings are futile, for in that universe the concepts of reason and freedom, which are at the heart of the tragic classical vision, are, probably, illusions; the reality is a massive, incomprehensible impersonality that manifests itself in the will of Juno.

The Dido Episode

Barbara J. Bono

The following analysis of the Aeneas-Dido episode charts the subtle dialectical process through which the narrator struggles to gain for us [a] perspective, to create [an] equilibrium. After we are given some broad indication of the tensions that inform the *Aeneid,* the meeting of Aeneas and Dido at first seems to offer a resolution. However, it is shadowed by a shared tragic past and the complex responses that past elicits. Aeneas's groping account of the unspeakable horror of the fall of Troy conveys the dimensions of historical change, of divine and human upheaval, that he must try to contain. At the moment he can do so only through retrospective narrative; enacting a solution must be deferred, in large part beyond his lifetime. His tale conveys both his sensitivity and his necessary detachment. Tragically, Dido responds only to the former, ignoring the latter. The indirection of the sequence, its imagery and divine machinery, depicts both the confluence and divergence of their minds, their individual ways of responding to change and history. The lovers are, to a point, complementary images, and it is only the harsh extremism of the world Virgil envisions that tears them apart. Later commentators and imitators who polarize them—sentimentalizing her, chilling and flattening him—distort the poet's truth. A complete resolution to the poem requires imagining another world.

The opening lines of the *Aeneid* hint at the great temporal, spatial, and spiritual distances to be explored and the form that may comprehend

From *Literary Transvaluation: From Vergilian Epic to Shakespearean Tragicomedy.* © 1984 by the Regents of the University of California. University of California Press, 1984.

them. From Troy to Italy, over sea and land, from the first man through his dynasty, at the mercy of a high, mysterious wrath that is named but not fully explained as mythic Juno, both driven and drawn on by fate, a man is racked until he becomes a symbolic architecture, a culture as well as a place, "altae moenia Romae," ("the walls of lofty Rome" 1.7). [All citations from the *Aeneid,* and their translations, are from *Virgil in Two Volumes,* trans. H. Rushton Fairclough, Loeb Classical Library, rev. ed., 2 vols.] The questioning of that wrath and the description of its lashing storm map in swift, broad, largely discontinuous strokes the many layers of the poem the narrator must labor to unite. Juno's fury flashes forward and backward in time, ahead to the rivalry of Carthage and Rome, back to the sources of the Trojan War. Yet even these sweeping historical explanations are made to seem, in their primitive anthropomorphism, inadequate to the narrator's metaphysical probing, "tantaene animis caelestibus irae?" ("Can resentment so fierce dwell in heavenly breasts?" 1.11). Virgil exposes from the first the strain between his inherited Homeric-Olympian form and his sophisticated philosophical sensibility. The characterization of Juno here juxtaposes abruptly the petty and the monumental, her envy of Pallas with the evocative, portentous "Talia flammato secum dea corde volutans" ("Thus inwardly brooding with heart inflamed" 1.50), in a way that foreshadows the poem's later psychological synthesis of the detailed and the significant. The maneuverings of the gods are elaborated with a strangely literalizing human political language—the indication that Aeolus is a corrupt constitutional monarch (1.50–64), the interplay between the serene description of Neptune and the constricting simile of the noble orator (1.148–56)—that at once reminds us of the contemporary, practical application of this work and forces that relationship. In short, the scope of the poem is arbitrarily, authoritatively laid down, outlined discursively, not yet created, not yet explained.

We then move to the human center on whom these events converge, and to his attempts to interpret them. At once we feel how crushingly this burden descends on him and the overwhelming nostalgia it evokes. In an instant the Trojans' clear purpose is disrupted; darkness and death rule; the ships are swept and battered from every direction. The line of resistance to these forces is the weakest anywhere in the poem, a supplicating figure whose words imply almost complete surrender. Aeneas's only detachment here is the knowledge that he did not die at Troy, which at this moment seems to have "saved" him for a meaningless death, alienated from native land, kin, and his own creative power. His first speech offers us immediate insight into his fragility. The events that follow and his second speech demonstrate how that weakness can be turned gradually into a source of strength.

Aeneas is upheld by a sense of responsibility to his past and the remnant of it he carries with him. As an individual he wishes he could die; as a leader he endures. As soon as the Trojan remnant lands communal activity starts: the men are "Aeneadae" ("sons of Aeneas" 1.157); his faithful friend Achates begins the rituals of civilization, and then accompanies his leader on a search for food and their lost comrades. Aeneas's deeply moving address—"O socii" ("O comrades" 1.198–207)—is his first attempt to shape the past through memory in order to sustain the future. Alluding here briefly to the tragic history he will later "feast" on ("pascit" 1.464) at the Carthaginian temple wall and then "revive" ("renovare" 2.3) at Dido's banquet, he urges his men to try to sublimate these sufferings to re-creation:

> "revocate animos maestumque timorem
> mittite; forsan et haec olim meminisse iuvabit.
> per varios casus, per tot discrimina rerum
> tendimus in Latium, sedes ubi fata quietas
> ostendunt; illic fas regna resurgere Troiae.
> durate, et vosmet rebus servate secundis."

"Recall your courage and put away sad fear. Perchance even this distress it will some day be a joy to recall. Through divers mishaps, through so many perilous chances, we fare towards Latium, where the fates point out a home of rest. There 'tis granted to Troy's realm to rise again; endure, and keep yourselves for days of happiness."

(1.202–7)

His speech builds through the warm, mounting internal pressure of the murmuring and sibilant alliteration, the careful architecture of the building phrases and sustaining imperatives. However, the re-creation is not yet convincing to Aeneas; he feigns ("simulat" 1.209) hope. The narrative leaves the human plane with the Trojan remnant "spemque metumque inter *dubii*" ("between hope and fear *uncertain*" 1.218), with *uncertainty* obscuring both the preceding clause and the entire episode.

The poem then moves to Jupiter's great proleptic speech, which theoretically resolves the entire action ("iam finis erat"; "now all was ended" 1.223), as Jupiter looks forth from the most inclusive perspective ("aethere summo"; "from the sky's summit" 1.223). It is authoritative, but also premature and unconvincing. The central significance of the succeeding encounter with Dido is to show Aeneas's difficult attainment of an approximation of this Jovial perspective from within the experience of rending change, the human forging of that consciousness, as faith rather than certainty, and as need rather than divine dictate. Virgil does so by detailing the historical and psychological depth of the tragic past and Aeneas's aesthetic removal from it, set against a sympathetic portrait of Dido's loss of such critical distance. Books 1 through 4 prove Aeneas a man of feeling even while the narrative of Dido's fall elaborates why his is a sensitivity necessarily deferred. The episode implies, through the hero, and for the narrator and the prospective audience, a humane sensibility that attempts to compassionate the frequently grim work of history.

The remainder of book 1 is couched as a gradual descent from Jove's perspective to an anatomy of human need. It opens the way for Aeneas's account of all he has lost. The apparent balance between Aeneas and Dido at their first meeting is subtly undermined by the strength of feeling they arouse in each other, a tension mounting throughout this book, climaxing in the wonderfully atmospheric hunt scene of book 4. These early passages also offer a few hints of the momentous differences between Aeneas's and Dido's responses to that release of feeling, differences that lead to those stark misunderstandings in books 4 and 6, to their divergent destinies: he will undergo catharsis as he gives way ("cessi" 2.804) and is stilled ("quievit" 3.718), while she will be wasted ("carpitur" 4.2), consumed.

The emotional undercurrent swells as Virgil moves us, first descriptively, then dramatically, first to Dido, then to Aeneas, toward the epiphanic encounter of the lovers. We start with the assurance that Dido, although "ignorant of fate" ("ne fati nescia" 1.299), has been favorably disposed toward the Trojans by Jove. But our first evidence of that gracious purpose, the commemorative temple frieze, is highly colored by emotion. We see the frieze through the eyes of Aeneas, who has not only experienced the horrors the panels depict but also has been slyly conditioned by his mother to see those panels as an expression of Dido's intimate sympathy. "'O sola infandos Troiae miserata labores'" ("'O thou that alone hast pitied Troy's unutterable woes'" 1.597), he exclaims.

Nor does it seem that his interpretation is exaggerated, for Dido's first speech to him stresses their community in suffering and desire:

"me quoque per multos similis fortuna labores
iactatam hac demum voluit consistere terra.
non ignara mali miseris succerrere disco."

"Me, too, has a like fortune driven through many toils, and
willed that at last I should find rest in this land. Not ignorant
of ill do I learn to befriend the unhappy."

(1.628–30)

Although Dido here maintains the Jovial balance, we sense within her a
vulnerability on which Venus will play. In these first scenes longing
continually threatens to burst through propriety. When Dido hears Ili-
oneus, she is "voltum demissa" ("with downcast face" 1.561)—is it
because of royal shame at his accusation of barbarism, or because of an
unexpected yearning toward the heroic Aeneas he describes? When
Aeneas's heart "rises"—"surgit" 1.582, the verb that also describes ris-
ing city walls—is it with vague hope, or a more definite ambition toward
this queen, this city?

Indeed, these unsuspected springs of feeling, human in expression
yet cosmic in origin and scope, that well up under the surface of this
regal encounter are complemented by the prominence of Venus, working
in book 1 independently of Jove. At the same time the differences be-
tween Aeneas's and Dido's experience of and reaction to Venus's inter-
vention foreshadow the divergent action to come.

Despite Jove's firm assurance that "'manent immota tuorum / fata
tibi'" ("'thy children's fates abide unmoved'" 1.257–58), Venus cannot
resist covertly tightening the ties that bind Aeneas and Dido, adding to
social bonds emotional and physical ones. As Aeneas approaches Car-
thage, Venus abruptly appears to him, disguised as a maiden huntress,
seemingly chaste, but in fact an agent of desire. She asks him if he has
seen one of her sisters, a question designed to make him look for another
like her; and so Dido will first appear, Diana-like, at the temple:

qualis in Eurotae ripis aut per iuga Cynthi
exercet Diana choros, quam mille secutae
hinc atque hinc glomerantur Oreades; illa pharetram
fert umero gradiensque deas supereminet omnis;
Latonae tacitum pertemptant gaudia pectus:
talis erat Dido, talem se laeta ferebat
per medios, instans operi regnisque futuris.

> Even as on Eurotas' banks or along the heights of Cynthus
> Diana guides her dancing bands, in whose train a thousand
> Oreads troop to right and left; she bears a quiver on her
> shoulder, and as she treads overtops all the goddesses; joys
> thrill Latona's silent breast—such was Dido, so moved she
> joyously through their midst, pressing on the work of her
> rising kingdom.
>
> (1.498–504)

Venus seems to prepare Aeneas to enter a realm of self-contained Amazonian women, but she also insinuates a more complex and sympathetic portrait of Dido as a woman of tragic experience, like his own, now turned to triumphant achievement. In book 1 Venus's affecting description of Dido's trials is a cue sufficient to elicit from Aeneas a complaining summary of his troubles; later, at Dido's urgings, he will give a full account that involves her totally in his pain. Venus has modulated Aeneas's nascent feelings for Dido from respect toward desire.

Here Aeneas is moved, unbalanced, but not completely deceived. Although Venus appears to him in human guise, he is her son ("Veneris" 1.325), attentive to the depths of feeling she sets in motion, wary, in short, of the numinous. He senses she is a goddess, although he does not know which one until, as she leaves him, she glancingly reveals herself. Immediately, the effect of their meeting is to heighten for Aeneas the attractiveness of Dido's present achievement in comparison with the elusiveness of his own desire. "'O fortunati, quorum iam moenia surgunt!'" ("'Happy they whose walls already rise!'" 1.437), he exclaims as he looks over Carthage. The intensity of his desire is revealed by his lament:

> ille ubi matrem
> adgnovit, tali fugientem est voce secutus:
> "quid natum totiens, crudelis tu quoque, falsis
> ludis imaginibus? cur dextrae iungere dextram
> non datur ac veras audire et reddere voces?"
> talibus incusat gressumque ad mòenia tendit.

> He knew her as his mother, and as she fled pursued her with
> these words: "Thou also cruel! Why mockest thou thy son so
> often with vain phantoms? Why am I not allowed to clasp
> hand in hand and hear and utter words unfeigned?" Thus he
> reproaches her and bends his steps towards the city.
>
> (1.405–10)

The full significance of the imagery of this lament becomes clearer as the poem unfolds and we see Aeneas's vain attempt to grasp two other phantoms, Creusa and Anchises. Aeneas yearns for his mother, his father, and his Trojan past more than for Dido. Once he recognizes them through tragic memory as irrevocably lost he will derive from that knowledge the desperate strength to revive them in appropriate forms; "'hoc opus, hic labor est'" ("'This is the task, this the toil!'" 6.129), cries the Sibyl of this strenuous resurrection, this ascent from the dead. The sympathetic respite offered by Dido allows him to move toward this recognition, as he gratefully acknowledges to the end (4.331–36). But insofar as she identifies with his past, he must finally leave her behind as well, just as he has left Troy; nostalgia, will, and pleasure must yield to his responsibility to re-create his people (4.340–61). Adam Parry has remarked in another context on the "sense of pregnant greatness in every detail of experience . . . impressed on us by the rhetorical exaggeration which pervades the *Aeneid*. . . . The potentialities of ages and empires . . . alive in the smallest details." So it is with the great longing revealed in Aeneas at this moment.

Ominously, Dido has no comparable recognition of how she is being affected by Venus. At the end of book 1 the goddess again works through a disguise, this time substituting her son Cupid for Aeneas's son, Ascanius. The picture of Dido unknowingly fondling the great god on her lap and bosom fuses the intimate sexual and maternal longings the handsome, heroic, and pious Aeneas has aroused in her. Ascanius is not only a surrogate son, but the image of his father.

> aut gremio Ascanium, genitoris imagine capta,
> detinet, infandum si fallere possit amorem.

> Captivated by his father's look, she holds Ascanius on her lap,
> if so she may beguile a passion beyond all utterance.
>
> (4.84–85)

Dido's tragedy in large part results from the surprising strength of these two strains of feeling curtailing the continued growth of a comparable piety in her; she falls from the initial "gentle mind and gracious purpose" ("animum mentemque benignam" 1.304) implanted in her by Jove to be victimized by the erotic and dynastic maneuverings of Venus and Juno. She indicates a limited human consciousness of this surrender in book 4 in her persistent qualms about unfaithfulness to Sychaeus and her disastrous clouding of the precise status of her relationship to Aeneas.

However, the language in which this access of love for Aeneas is described in book 1 indicates that it comes upon her as a surprise, deceitfully, from an act of friendship which she suddenly cannot dissociate from her very identity. Dido's own description of this development, at the beginning of book 4, relates her fall to the just-recounted fall of Troy.

Dido's tragedy forms the generic link between Homeric epic and the world Virgil depicts. She thinks she can welcome Aeneas according to the archaic code of guest-friendship, remaining faithful to Sychaeus while forwarding her own masculine heroic endeavor. Yet Venus harbors a great disingenuousness in her admiring exclamation, "'dux femina facti'" ("'the leader of the work a woman'" 1.364), for Dido is not only female but the embodiment of an archetypal "femaleness" (in which Aeneas also participates) that in its emotional capacity and vulnerability indicates the need for something other than the Homeric active *virtú*. Dido is not another Odysseus, single-handedly capable of restoring the past, although she has struggled "manfully" to fill the part. Venus exposes her need, which Dido mistakenly looks to a heroic Aeneas to fulfill. We see the seeds of her misapprehension perhaps as early as the description of the temple frieze, which, although it portrays the sufferings of all the Trojans, depicts Aeneas in vigorous battle, "se quoque principibus permixtum adgnovit Achivis" ("Himself too, in close combat with the Achaean chiefs, he recognized" 1.488). Certainly Venus's miraculous introduction of the hero, not a bedraggled shipwreck, but "claraque in luce refulsit, / os umerosque deo similis" ("gleaming in the clear light, godlike in face and shoulders" 1.588–89), fuels Dido's need, which then ignites at the banquet. Aeneas's account of the fall of Troy should reveal clearly that he too is a tragic victim whose heroism must consist in suffering as well as action. However, the distance between his weary detachment and Dido's passionate engagement with the past implicitly widens throughout his narration, until in book 4 she is as a figure from Euripidean tragedy, overthrown by irrational forces surging beneath the fragile forms of civilization.

Dido is "fired" by Aeneas's account into a precipitate action that entails the destruction of herself and, eventually, her city. (See 1.659–60, 688, 713; 4.1–2, 23, 54, 65–69, 300, 360, 364, 669–71, and 697 for the metaphor of passion as flame, a metaphor whose climax appears in the comparison of her suicide and the conflagration of the city.) Believing she can reinstate the Homeric world of active heroism, she actually recapitulates its demise. She does not perceive the distance between the rending force of the events Aeneas has endured—events that have deprived him of the powers of action—and the tentative meaning he gives them in his narration. She is alive to his tale of tragic horror as if it were epic deed. Blind desire causes her to idealize his former heroism even while absorbing his shattered emotional condition. Taking on his fears, she now becomes fearful, transformed from the assured lawgiver to the doubt-torn listener of these lines, feasting her soul uncritically on another's "unsubstantial picture" that evokes their common memory of loss and travail:

> incipit effari, mediaque in voce resistit;
> nunc eadem labente die convivia quaerit,
> Iliacosque iterum demens audire labores
> exposcit pendetque iterum narrantis ab ore.

She essays to speak and stops with the word half-spoken. Now, as day wanes, she seeks that same banquet, again madly craves to hear the sorrows of Ilium and again hangs on the speaker's lips.

(4.76–79)

Dido's revelations to Anna at the beginning of book 4 offer the first direct testimony to her inner state; her words shock us in their similarity to Aeneas's account of the fall of Troy.

> "Anna soror, *quae me suspensam insomnia terrent!*
> *quis novus hic nostris successit sedibus hospes,*
> quem sese ore ferens, quam forti pectore et armis!
> credo equidem, nec vana fides, genus esse deorum.
> degeneres animos timor arguit. heu! quibus ille
> iactatus fatis! quae bella exhausta canebat!
> si mihi non animo fixum immotumque sederet,
> ne cui me vinclo vellem sociare iugali,
> postquam primus amor deceptam morte fefellit:
> si non pertaesum thalami taedaeque fuisset,
> huic uni forsan potui succumbere culpae.
> Anna, fatebor enim, miseri post fata Sychaei
> coniugis et sparsos fraterna caede Penatis
> *solus hic inflexit sensus animumque labantem*
> *impulit, adgnosco veteris vestigia flammae.*"

"Anna, my sister, *what dreams thrill me with fears? Who is this stranger guest that hath entered our home?* How noble his mien!

how brave in heart and feats of arms! I believe it well—nor is assurance vain—that he is sprung from gods. 'Tis fear that proves souls base-born. Alas! by what fates is he vexed! What wars, long endured, did he recount! Were the purpose not planted in my mind, fixed and immovable, to ally myself with none in bond of wedlock, since my first love, turning traitor, cheated me by death; were I not utterly weary of the bridal bed and torch, to this one weakness, perchance, I might have yielded! Anna—for I will own it—since the death of my hapless lord Sychaeus, and the shattering of our home by a brother's murder, *he alone has swayed my will and overthrown my tottering soul. I recognize the traces of the olden flame.*"

(4.9–23; emphasis mine)

The dreams that thrill her with fears recall Aeneas's alarm at the dream vision of Hector; her language echoes Aeneas's uncertainty at the moment of exile, "'nunc omnes terrent aurae, sonus excitat omnis / suspensum et pariter comitique onerique timentem'" ("'I now am affrighted by every breeze and startled by every sound, tremulous as I am and fearing alike for my companion and my burden'" 2.728–29). The "stranger guest" who has entered her home ominously suggests the treachery of Sinon, the encroaching wooden horse, and Pyrrhus threatening at the palace gates. Dido's reluctance to violate the cherished image of her first husband, Sychaeus, recalls the total devastation Pyrrhus wreaks. Her picture of her will swayed, her tottering soul overthrown, is like the Trojans' desperate toppling of the citadel, "'adgressi ferro circum, qua summa labantis / iuncturas tabulata dabant, convellimus altis / sedibus impulimusque'" ("'Assailing this with iron round about, where the top-most stories offered weak joints, we wrenched it from its lofty place and thrust it forth'" 2.463–65). She becomes the last in a line of tragic figures whose self-sufficiency is shattered by the great fall into time and experience the Trojan War represents. In a heart-rending irony, "pius" Aeneas, its latest victim, becomes her unwitting Pyrrhus.

Most sadly, her fall is finally depicted as something she could not resist, as an imprisonment in a more primitive cast of mind. She loses the aesthetic detachment represented by the temple frieze and celebrated by Aeneas there, to enter that tragic picture,

> Penthesilea furens mediisque in milibus ardet,
> aurea subnectens exsertae cingula mammae,
> bellatrix, audetque viris concurrere virgo.

Penthesilea in fury leads the crescent-shielded ranks of the Amazons and rages amid her thousands; a golden belt binds her naked breast, while she, a warrior queen, dares battle, a maid clashing with men.

(1.491–93)

To Dido's unconscious overthrow by Venus is added her uncritical allegiance to Juno, which creates a level of tragic self-deceit in her liaison with Aeneas and turns it from friendship to bitter enmity. Driven by passion, but genuinely concerned lest she do something shameful and covert, she tries to legitimate the transfer of her affections from the dead Sychaeus to Aeneas by appealing to the gods, and particularly to Juno, "vincla iugalia curae" ("guardian of wedlock bonds" 4.59). Yet the "answer" she receives is not a prompting to confront him openly and resolve the ambiguities of the situation. Instead, she loses the rational powers of speech—"nunc media Aenean secum per moenia ducit / Sidoniasque ostentat opes urbemque paratam; / *incipit effari, mediaque in voce resistit*" ("Now through the city's midst she leads with her Aeneas, and displays her Sidonian wealth and the city built; *she essays to speak and stops with the word half-spoken*" 4.74–76, emphasis mine). The action then moves to the plane of the deities, where we witness the colloquy of Venus and Juno.

For her part, Juno promises to confirm a valid marriage for the pair with Jupiter, but then does not, because she knows he would forbid it. Still trying to circumvent the decrees of Fate, she presides at a charged, intimate, "inevitable" meeting that Dido can, although not without misgivings, interpret as a marriage (4.166–72), or at least as one begun (4.316, 431), while Aeneas remains innocent of these meanings (4.337–39). Juno's willfulness ensures that of Dido, who allows herself to be swept along by events rather than choosing them, shaping them. She shows a pathetic, partial awareness that she is losing self-control, but that lack of control results from the crude maneuverings of the powerful primitive gods she worships. She is stage-managed by them, until she is like a Bacchante (4.68–69, 300–303), or a tragic figure hounded by the chthonic gods:

> Eumenidum veluti demens videt agmina Pentheus
> et solem geminum et duplices se ostendere Thebas,
> aut Agamemnonius scaenis agitatus Orestes
> armatam facibus matrem et serpentibus atris
> cum fugit, ultricesque sedent in limine Dirae.

Even as raving Pentheus sees the Furies' band, a double sun and two-fold Thebes rise to view; or as when Agamemnon's son, Orestes, driven over the stage, flees from his mother, who is armed with brands and black serpents, while at the doorway crouch the avenging Fiends.

(4.469–73)

These two similes, by referring to classical Greek tragedy, specify exactly Dido's situation. They place her in that tragic moment of history and consciousness that succeeded the era of the Homeric epics, and that it is the task of Virgilian epic to overcome. Her bitter confrontation with the departing Aeneas reveals stark differences between their individual conceptions of the gods. She taunts him for his providential beliefs while appealing more and more ominously to the chthonic aspects of the gods who have betrayed her, to "Erebumque Chaosque / tergeminamque Hecaten, tria virginis ora Dianae" ("Erebus and Chaos, and threefold Hecate, triple-faced maiden Diana" 4.510–11); to "'Sol, qui terrarum flammis opera omnia lustras, / tuque harum interpres curarum et conscia Iuno, / nocturnisque Hecate triviis ululata per urbes / et Dirae ultrices et di morientis Elissae'" ("'O Sun, who with thy beams surveyest all the works of earth, and thou, Juno, mediatress and witness of these my sorrows, and Hecate, whose name is shrieked by night at the crossroads of cities, ye avenging Furies, and ye gods of dying Elissa'" 4.607–10); and even to "'sacra Iove *Stygio*'" ("the rites of *Stygian* Jove'" 4.638, emphasis mine). Finally, she immerses herself in a form of sympathetic black magic that draws her to suicide. It is Juno who has become "omnipotens" (4.693) in her life and who at last offers her a pitying release from it.

Dido may imagine that she could have remained faithful to the values of her old world; her final speech celebrates her heroic identity before Aeneas's advent:

"vixi et, quem dederat cursum Fortuna, peregi,
et nunc magna mei sub terras ibit imago.
urbem praeclaram statuia, mea moenia vidi,
ulta virum poenas inimico a fratre recepi,
felix, heu! nimium felix, si litora tantum
numquam Dardaniae tetigissent nostra carinae!"

"I have lived, I have finished the course that Fortune gave; and now in majesty my shade shall pass beneath the earth. A noble city I have built; my own walls I have seen; avenging my husband, I have exacted punishment from my brother and foe—happy, ah! too happy, had but the Dardan keels never touched our shores!"

(4.653–58)

In the underworld, where "'quisque suos patimur Manis'" ("'Each of us suffers his own spirit'" 6.743), she is allowed to revert to this former shadowy ideal, denying Aeneas's vision. But in fact he did touch her shores, bringing with him a wider historical perspective on human action. Unable to distance her sympathy from immediate gratification, she is swept away with Aeneas's old world, "'non ignara mali'" ("'not ignorant of ill'" 1.630), yet "ne fati nescia" ("ignorant of fate" 1.299). In the values of her own archaic heroic code she is blameworthy, but he is "perfide" ("false" 4.305, 366), "improbe" ("shameless" 4.386), "hostem" ("foe" 4.424). Yet in the code of values developed in the *Aeneid* he would be blameworthy if he stayed, and is "pius" (4.393) in going, while she is "infelix" ("unhappy" 1.712, 749; 4.68, 450), "inscia" ("unknowing" 1.718), "misera ante diem subitoque accensa furore ("hapless before her day, and fired by sudden madness" 4.697), the victim of "casu . . . iniquo" ("unjust doom" 6.475).

Thus the meeting of Dido and Aeneas illustrates Virgil's vision of a former heroic ideal set against a tragic world of experience, and the resulting gulf of mutual misinterpretation. In book 1, at the temple, Aeneas and Dido seem to meet as the lucid, assured controllers of destiny, two demigods; covertly they are drawn together in the shadowy, nervous dependence of fate's victims. Each will clutch at a premature, false security in the other, to awake with shock to the elemental feelings they expose. In book 4 we are moved by the immense creative potential of their union. In a setting aglow with morning light, replete with the bursting yet purposive energy of the hunt, the Queen comes forth.

> tandem progreditur magna stipante caterva.
> Sidoniam picto chlamydem circumdata limbo.
> cui pharetra ex auro, crines nodantur in aurum,
> aurea purpuream subnectit fibula vestem.
> nec non et Phyrgii comites et laetus Iulus
> incedunt; ipse ante alios pulcherrimus omnis
> infert se socium Aeneas atque agmina iungit.
> qualis ubi hibernam Lyciam Xanthique fluenta
> deserit ac Delum maternam invisit Apollo

> instauratque choros, mixtique altaria circum
> Cretesque Dryopesque fremunt pictique Agathyrsi;
> ipse iugis Cynthi graditur mollique fluentem
> fronde premit crinem fingens atque implicat auro
> tela sonant umeris: haud illo segnior ibat
> Aeneas, tantum egregio decus enitet ore.

At last she comes forth, attended by a mighty throng, and clad in a Sidonian robe with embroidered border. Her quiver is of gold, her tresses are knotted into gold, golden is the buckle to clasp her purple cloak. With her pace a Phrygian train and joyous Iülus. Aeneas himself, goodly beyond all others, advances to join her and unites his band with hers. As when Apollo quits Lycia, his winter home, and the streams of Xanthus, to visit his mother's Delos, and renews the dance, while mingling about his altars Cretans and Dryopes and painted Agathyrsians raise their voices—he himself treads the Cynthian ridges, and with soft leafage shapes and binds his flowing locks, braiding it with golden diadem; the shafts rattle on his shoulders: so no less lightly than he went Aeneas, such beauty shines forth from his noble face!

(4.136–50)

The chief impression conveyed by this emphatically celebratory, luminous description is masterful control of tremendous energy. The swelling simile comparing Aeneas to Apollo arches back to draw in the earlier magnificent comparison of Dido to Diana (1.498–506). And again, the sheer vividness and amplitude of the picture presses the simile temporarily into a statement of fact; for a moment we actually believe we are in the presence of the twin deities. Besides glorifying the radiant appearance of the lovers, this image of Aeneas and Dido suggests they are like brother and sister, the sun-god and the virginal huntress, and thus seems to deny the sexual nature of their attraction.

But ominous foreshadowings hint that this appearance of sexual aloofness masks volatile sexual longing. Dido first lingers in her bedroom ("thalamo" 4.133), and Venus earlier appeared to Aeneas in Diana-like disguise to plant surreptitiously the seeds of love. Earlier images of hunting have modulated toward sympathy for the victim. In book 1 Aeneas the leader felled a troop of deer (1.184–93), and Dido is like a maiden huntress (1.314–417 and 498–506). Now Dido in love has become an unwary hind wounded by an unknowing shepherd (4.68–73). The vaunting lovers who commence this hunt will soon, like animals, be driven to ground in the "nuptial" cave (4.160–72). Similarly ambiguous are the rich gold and purple accoutrements that adorn the tresses of Dido and of Aeneas-as-Apollo. At first these diadems seem images of control, but in the larger symbolism of the poem, the Asiatic richness of Dido's kingdom is portrayed as a temptation to lawless indulgence.

On the surface, then, this passage intensifies and joins the two previous ideal images that the lovers had of each other, and allows us to see the possibilities of their union as triumphant spectacle; the energies and accomplishments of the two peoples flow together, civilization crowns striving, and the succession from the united races seems favorably determined by Dido's loving acceptance of the Trojan heir, Iülus-Ascanius. But the crosscurrents are stronger, pointing to Virgil's fears of the causes that act in history. Juno's storm breaks, scattering the company and plunging the lovers into an obscure union from which Dido never emerges, from which Aeneas must absolve himself. To Virgil's tragic sense of history, providential shaping powers are not accessible to individuals. They are only available indirectly through them to communities and institutions. Unlike the Neoplatonic Egyptian triumphal union envisioned by the lovers in Shakespeare's *Antony and Cleopatra,* in the *Aeneid* the differences between the reasons and powers of the gods and those of men are too marked to be bridged by a ladder of gradual ascent in understanding. Any imaginative ideal is severely tested by the material conditions that encourage or inhibit its possible fulfillment. In Shakespeare's Egypt these conditions—geography, flora and fauna, and human culture—support Antony and Cleopatra's imaginative ideal of eternal erotic union. Conversely, Aeneas's providential mission subordinates the material reality of Dido and Carthage to the projected reality of Rome; indeed, Aeneas experiences this material reality as a powerful drag on his ideal. Thus material conditions, which in Shakespeare's play can serve as metaphors for the divine, immanent signs of transcendence, are in Virgil's world temptations to be refined through renunciation into more extensive ideals.

Book 2 is the crucible of the *Aeneid,* the great trial from which the painful solutions of the poem are forged. In it Aeneas, speaking "ab alto" (2.2) "revives" the fall of Troy, articulating fully the experience of loss already epitomized at 1.92–101 and 1.446–93. We witness his descent into a realm of shifting experience, of history, and its meaning for him. As a hallowed old world dies and a new world struggles to be born, events and language used to describe them darken from realistic to symbolic, from formulaic architecture to Virgilian mannerism. Aeneas becomes a new kind of hero, or even an antihero, deprived of the ability to impose his own ordering on the world through the exercise of *arête*. He is now enduring Aeneas, the patient *sufferer*, the *medium* of Roman destiny. Virgil explicitly shows, through the change wrought in Aeneas on the night of Troy's fall, the transition from Homeric to Virgilian hero.

Aeneas remembers Troy on the night of its fall as a shadowy labyrinth of terrifying apparitions and irreversible events that constrained action and heightened emotion. He feels himself pressed inward both physically and psychologically as first he realizes that the walls of the city have been breached by deceit, then that the palace is under attack, then that even this last stronghold is pierced to its very heart. Early in the horrible night Aeneas leaps to battle like a Homeric hero, "'furor iraque mentem / praecipitant, pulchrumque mori succurrit in armis'" ("'Rage and wrath drive my soul headlong and I think how glorious it is to die in arms'" 2.316–17). Soon he is deprived of such certainties, as he first follows the counsel of Coroebus by adopting Greek deceit, wearing their arms (2.370–401), only to have the ruse turn on his company when they are conterattacked by the Trojans. The inevitability of Troy's fall is focused in the picture of the frantic defenders themselves tearing down their city,

> "Dardanidae contra turris ac tecta domorum
> culmina convellunt; his se, quando ultima cernunt,
> extrema iam in morte parant defendere telis;
> auratasque trabes, veterum decora illa parentum,
> devolvunt."

> "The Trojans in turn tear down the towers and roof-covering of the palace; with these as missiles—for they see the end near—even at the point of death they prepare to defend themselves; and roll down gilded rafters, the splendours of their fathers of old."

(2.445–49)

The destruction is complete when, from the roof of the palace, Aeneas must helplessly watch the sacrilegious murder of Priam by Achilles' son Pyrrhus. Pyrrhus has reached the source of the city, the shrine of the gods, fountain of vitality for old Priam and his many children who, in the "'famous fifty chambers,'" had formerly fulfilled the "'rich promise of offspring'" ("'quinquaginta illi thalami, spes tanta nepotum'" 2.503). The seeds of Troy, instead of being honored in the city's deep recesses as fire on the altars of the gods and as the spark of generating life in the bodies of Troy's people, are now released and scattered by Pyrrhus's desecrating act.

This intensely personal and yet symbolic account concludes with a shocking monumental image: Priam "'once lord of so many tribes and lands, the monarch of Asia,'" now "'lies a huge trunk upon the shore, a head severed from the shoulders, a nameless corpse!'" ("'tot quondam populis terrisque superbum / regnatorem Asiae. iacet ingens litore truncus, / avolsumque umeris caput et sine nomine corpus'" 2.556–58). The death of the carefully characterized king, frail yet also kindly, paternal, noble, and sacral, symbolizes the fall of his city and his civilization. The narrative discontinuity—a moment earlier he was described as thrust through the side, not decapitated—only serves to heighten the significance of the final image of an edifice demolished, a huge tree cut down. The image of the fallen tree is fully expanded in the apocalyptic vision of 2.626–31, only to be reversed at the climactic moment of book 4.

Although Aeneas is made to suffer with his city, he survives its destruction. While moving inward, he also moves upward, gaining perspective and a shocked, raw understanding in proportion to his helplessness to act. His experience of the death throes of Troy gives an immediate, human meaning to Hector's original warning to flee; the spectacle of Priam dead prompts memory of his father, wife, and child:

> "At me tum primum saevus circumstetit horror.
> obstipui; subiit cari genitoris imago,
> ut regem aequaevum crudeli volnere vidi
> vitam exhalantem; subiit deserta Creusa
> et direpta domus et parvi casus Iuli."

> "Then first an awful horror encompassed me. I stood aghast, and there rose before me the form of my dear father, as I looked upon the king, of like age, gasping away his life under a cruel wound. There rose forlorn Creüsa, the pillaged house, and the fate of little Iülus."

> (2.559–63)

He recalls them tenderly: his father "cari," his wife "deserta," his son "parvi." For Aeneas his love of a particular place, of particular people, must animate those prophecies that he receives, but whose precise shape he only dimly understands. At the same time, the awesome events of that night make familiar things mysteriously significant, a part of a much larger action. Venus appears, appealing to this intimate love and yet making clear the apocalyptic upheaval it must bridge: it is the gods themselves—only they are powerful enough—who bring down Troy (2.588–633). The counteraction, the founding of an adequate "new Troy," must be similarly portentous, similarly numinous, as the events at Anchises' house illustrate.

From that moment Aeneas begins to live for tomorrow and to rely on his family as a chain linking the sanctity of the past and the promise of the future. He feels himself fallen: as he flees he bears the descending symbolic structure of three earlier ages: the golden-age images of the gods themselves; his father, silver-age lover of Venus, representative of that blissful time when men spoke with gods as "friend with friend"; and his own bronze-age heroic image, tarnished, turned to iron, by the events of the night. Gradually, over the course of the entire poem, he will acquire hope in the mysteriously illuminated son he leads, and in the vague prophecies of another city that sharpen, even as they expand in significance to include both Greek and Trojan worlds, both Europe and Asia, both mythic past and glorious future. Now he is only at the beginning of that new phase of historical consciousness, "'suspensum et pariter comitique onerique timentem'" ("'tremulous . . . and fearing alike for my companion and burden'" 2.729).

The extent of what Aeneas has lost and the intensity of his feelings of loss reveal, then, not only the nature of his attraction to Dido but also the deeper impulses that prompt him to leave her. Deprived of the advice of his father, welcomed to Dido's realm—an event not mentioned in any of the prophecies—which combines veneration for the past with vigorous new energy, it is no wonder he lapses into quiescence at the end of his narration. Yet through recounting the fall of Troy he has obtained an initial perspective ("ab alto") on it, and from now on he is never as engaged with Dido as she is with him. He does not initiate action; while he shares in the fault of cohabiting with her, he does not deceive himself and others by terming it a marriage. He has portrayed his deepest love for the fallen Troy, and the remembered image reverberates, its pressure mounting subliminally, even as he thinks himself happy in Carthage. It surfaces in book 4, in both divine and human form, as the peremptory commands of Mercury, the hauntings by his father's ghost, his guilt toward Ascanius, and the imperative to create a new Troy (4.351–61). The movement of his reply to Dido reveals how the sympathy she of-

fered, the elegiac images she conjured in the temple frieze and the re-
peatedly evoked narration of the fall of Troy function to define his
mission of self-sacrifice.

> "me si fata meis paterentur ducere vitam
> auspiciis et sponte mea componere curas,
> urbem Troianam primum dulcisque meorum
> reliquias colerem, Priami tecta alta manerent,
> et recidiva manu posuissem Pergama victis.
> sed nunc Italiam magnam Gryneus Apollo,
> Italiam Lyciae iussere capessere sortes;
> hic amor, haec patria est. si te Karthaginis arces
> Phoenissam Libycaeque aspectus detinet urbis,
> quae tandem Ausonia Teucros considere terra
> invidia est? et nos fas extera quaerere regna."

"Did the Fates suffer me to shape my life after my own plea-
sure and order my sorrows at my own will, my first care
should be the city of Troy and the sweet relics of my kin.
Priam's high house would still abide and my own hand should
have set up a revived Pergamus for the vanguished. But now
of great Italy has Grynean Apollo bidden me lay hold, of Italy
the Lycian oracles. There is my love, there my country! If the
towers of Carthage and the sight of the Libyan city charm
thee, a Phoenician, why, pray, grudge the Trojans their settling
on Ausonian land? We, too, may well seek a foreign realm."
(4.340–50)

Even now he lingers over the sweet memory of Troy before assuming
the disciplined lockstep, "'nunc Italiam . . . Italiam . . . hic . . . haec
. . . est.'"

What seems insensitivity on his part is, on more careful exami-
nation, not the absence of feeling, but a suppression that obliquely shows
us how much Dido's tragedy is rooted in his, even as her tragedy propels
him beyond tragedy. The catastrophe he has experienced has forced him
to enlarge indefinitely the distance between emotion and action, between
what he can acknowledge in his words and in his deeds:

> Tandem pauca refert: "ego te, *quae plurima fando*
> *enumerare vales,* numquam, regina, negabo
> promeritam, *nec me meminisse pigebit Elissae,*

> dum memor ipse mei, dum spiritus hos regit artus.
> *pro re* pauca loquar.

> At last he briefly replies: "I will never deny, O Queen, that thou hast deserved of me *the utmost thou canst set forth in speech, nor shall my memory of Elissa be bitter,* while I have memory of myself, and while breath still sways these limbs. *For my course* few words will I say."

(4.333–37; emphasis mine)

It is their *mutual* tragedy that he cannot cherish, except in memory, what Dido so touchingly describes as what they had begun (4.314–19) and what might have been (4.327–29). His words here are a bleak attempt to reinstate the warmly sympathetic yet decorous initial relationship he earlier celebrated (1.595–610), before passion tipped that delicate balance toward impulsive action.

His sense of the sorrow of this leave-taking is actually *more* acute than hers, for his departure echoes the violence done him at the destruction of Troy. Now he must constrain her heroic identity to an object of memory, as he has already done with his own: "'nor shall my memory of Elissa be bitter, while I have memory of myself.'" Her sympathy for the suffering at Troy, "'sunt lacrimae rerum et mentem mortalia tangunt'" ("'here, too, there are tears for misfortune and mortal sorrows touch the heart'" 1.462), has become participation, and he mourns the compound tragedy even as he struggles to see these fated events as Jove does.

> Talibus orabat, talisque miserrima fletus
> fertque refertque soror. sed nullis ille movetur
> fletibus, aut voces ullas tractabilis audit;
> fata obstant, placidasque viri deus obstruit auris.
> ac velut annoso validam cum robore quercum
> Alpini Boreae nunc hinc nunc flatibus illinc
> eruere inter se certant; it stridor, et altae
> consternunt terram concusso stipite frondes;
> ipsa haeret scopulis et, quantum vertice ad auras
> aetherias, tantum radice in Tartara tendit:
> haud secus adsiduis hinc atque hinc vocibus heros
> tunditur, et magno persentit pectore curas;
> mens immota manet, lacrimae volvuntur inanes.

Such was her prayer and such the tearful pleas the unhappy

sister bears again and again. But by no tearful pleas is he moved, nor in yielding mood pays he heed to any words. Fate withstands and heaven seals his kindly, mortal ears. Even as when northern Alpine winds, blowing now hence, now thence, emulously strive to uproot an oak strong with the strength of years, there comes a roar, the stem quivers and the high leafage thickly strews the ground, but the oak clings to the crag, and as far as it lifts its top to the airs of heaven, so far it strikes its roots down towards hell—even so with ceaseless appeals, from this side and from that, the hero is buffeted, and in his mighty heart feels the thrill of grief: steadfast stands his will; the tears fall in vain.

(4.437–49)

Although Dido and Aeneas are apart, her tears and his tears flow together in a powerful strain of pity for mortal things that gives an elegiac cast to the entire poem, in which no single human life is large enough to encompass the upheavals depicted. At the same time, the simile of the oak tree—which is deliberately "rather too large for its setting" recalls the horrible visions of Priam fallen (1.512–14, 558–59) and Troy overthrown by the gods (1.626–29), and anticipates the *nekuia* and the introduction to Latium (7.59–67). The simile describes Aeneas as the organic medium through which the past will finally be resurrected in a more universal form. He is a life tree, uniting an archetypal primitive past with a more sophisticated, comprehensive culture. At this terrible moment the man and his mission are presented serially (his kindly mortal ears are made deaf by Fate, tears cannot conquer his will), but the simile of the great tree reminds us that his is a sacrifice made for human community. Aeneas has not destroyed his humanity, although he has had to drive it deeply underground, whence it emerges only fitfully in the troubled remaining course of the poem. Its proper expression remains his ideal, and the first third of the *Aeneid,* while illustrating the lovers' tragic disjunction, implies a future when leadership and fellow-feeling will not exert opposing claims, when historical responsibility will not require emotional sacrifice:

> "Romane, memento
> (hae tibi erunt artes) pacique imponere morem,
> parcere subiectis et debellare superbos."

"Remember thou, O Roman, to rule the nations with thy

sway—these shall be thine arts—to crown Peace with Law,
to spare the humbled, and to tame in war the proud!"
(6.851–53)

In short, the opening third of the poem attempts to effect a ca-
tharsis, to create a state of mind that can transcend tragedy instead of
being condemned to reenact it, that can transmute the primitive and
chthonic into the cultured and philosophic. The tragedy is conceived as
the failure of the Homeric world of self-contained, active heroism in the
face of overwhelming historical and emotional change. Dido's fall is the
psychological correlative of the fall of Troy, indeed of ancient civilization
in general. At the moment of Dido's suicide it was "quam si immissis
ruat hostibus omnis /Karthago aut *antiqua Tyros,* flammaeque furentes /
culmina perque hominum volvantur perque deorum" ("even as though
all Carthage or *ancient Tyre* were falling before the inrushing foe, and
fierce flames were rolling on over the roofs of men, over the roofs of
gods" 4.669–71, emphasis mine). Adopting much of the symbolic lan-
guage of Euripidean tragedy, Virgil shows Dido as a conduit for irrational
forces that swelled up outside and within the norms of Greek culture.
For Virgil this tragic experience is inevitable, and those caught in it must
attempt to constructively channel it through consciousness and over
time. This is Aeneas's mission; his seeming detachment does not so
much deny his feelings for Dido and his lost past as contain them, in
his memory, in his retrospective art, until they can find positive expres-
sion in a more ample and secure future. He knowingly sacrifices his self,
which otherwise would be destroyed by passion and time, to an as yet
indefinite collective destiny, and thus he turns personal tragedy into an
act of faith in his race. The poem as a whole attempts to prompt this
complex (many readers have said impossible) response in its audience;
we are to simultaneously acknowledge the pity and terror of these ancient
events and their effect as a means to a greater good.

The oppositions in the *Aeneid,* then, are not essentially posed as
alternatives, but rather as stages in a process whose evolution may surpass
the suggested solutions of the poem. The basic problem Virgil confronts
is that of historical change, of conflict in and enlargement of one's world
beyond expectations, and seemingly beyond the capacity of traditional
forms to contain or explain it. Virgil's Rome was undergoing just such
a change, and Virgil himself was involved in it—Actium was still a
recent event to counterweight centuries of the traumas of expansionism
and decades of civil war, and there was the persistent worry that the

Augustan peace might not outlast Octavius himself. Thus Virgil is as much concerned to present a method or attitude for encountering traumatic change as a definitive statement of its end. The latter must and does remain hypothetical or remote in the poem, a fact ignored by centuries of readers anxious to harden its fiction into orthodox meaning. Instead, Virgil proceeds dialectically; clear, painful, experiential knowledge of the inadequacies of the past is used to generate patient expectation; to deepen, strengthen, and expand the original ground of one's being, to enable it to support growth. Exile will be but the mode of a more triumphant return.

However, once this process is understood—in this poem there is no *direct* return to Troy, no possible unshadowed embrace with Dido—one must still confront squarely the immense cost for individual human beings. Dido, Turnus, and the other "primitive" figures in the poem simply cannot see their historical situation clearly enough to modify their desires accordingly. They live with a somewhat less than full consciousness of moral responsibility for their dilemmas; they feel this, and find themselves in a nightmare world of unspecified connections. They are offered a pale underworld consonant with this sense of constraint; can it compensate for their thwarted potential? As for Aeneas, whose way is only relatively more clear, can the glorious future prophesied for his descendents compensate for his self-sacrifice? One might respond that he will be rewarded with the bliss of the joyous fields or the gradual purifications of the cycle of reincarnation, but Aeneas's own question, "'quae lucis miseris tam dira cupido?' " ("'What means, alas! this their mad longing for the light?'" 6.721), resounds much more powerfully in the poem than Anchises' detached philosophical sermon.

In one sense, such objections are anachronistic and even sentimental. The type of individual freedom, the expressive will, we might want to champion for these characters is, for the most part, dispraised in the poem as the outmoded, destructive Homeric *arêté*. The major argument of the *Aeneid* is the necessary subordination of that individuality to the community, the state. The great images of the work—the tree, the hearth, the terrifying labyrinth domesticated as the productive beehive—figure it forth. Although these values may seem to us impersonal, monolithic, totalitarian, or fascistic, Virgil so roots them in familiar Roman life as to lend warmth to every detail of the *Aeneid*. Ancient man was not man without place and society. A deep reverence for traditional Roman landscape, ways, and values—the materials of the *Georgics* and book 8 of the *Aeneid*—suffuses the entire epic and provides the positive complement to the more dramatic, sweeping, historical and generic trag-edy that impels the poem. Indeed, one major strain of the interpretative tradition reduces the *Aeneid* to a glorification of things Roman.

As many of the best recent critics argue, Virgil consciously, pains-takingly writes his poem in opposition to the world of Homeric heroism. For our purposes, however, we must also point to the world he intimates but cannot yet bespeak. If the poem looks backward to the ancient world, it also looks forward to Christian eschatology. The *Aeneid* exposes an intensity of longing more dynamic and creative than nostalgia, one in which Troy, Carthage, and even Rome itself function less as places, as a set of material conditions, and more as metaphors for the ideal. And here we find ourselves, following Johnson and Auerbach, in an area of perpetually re-creative fictions, not unlike those of the Bible, where the repeated displacements, the "pendulations" of the text, the interpretive gaps it opens, oblige us to enter into completing them. This is where the *Aeneid* itself had to falter, and where a more personal creed like Christianity could enter and appropriate its rhythms. The "world" of the *Aeneid* did ultimately depend on the "conversion" of one man, Oc-tavius Augustus Caesar, yet he could not sustain it alone. The mystery, interiority, subjectivity of the text had to become explicit; the text recre-ated in every mind. The drama of consciousness had to become central; the epic, autobiography. The allegorical impulse inherent in the text (un-like the Homeric epics, for which the frequent allegorizations were largely imposed), its negative suggestion of "another world," could combine powerfully with Judaeo-Christian and Neoplatonic myths of exile and purified striving. Then further layers of meaning could be added to the text; then the world of the *Aeneid,* the Roman world, could itself be used, without violation of the basic structure of the text, as the basis for more spiritual values. Although . . . later authors could slight the dialectical process of the text in favor of a single-minded defense of one of its components, it is this process, Virgil's use of a tragic sensibility to define epic purpose, that is the most poignant index to the uncertainties of his times and his most complex legacy to the ages.

War and Peace

K. W. Gransden

In *Aeneid* 12 Virgil manipulates the roles of Hector and Achilles for the last time. In *Aeneid* 6 the Sibyl had foretold that a second Achilles already born in Latium would engage Aeneas in a second Trojan war. Thus Aeneas must become an avenging Hector, destined to reverse, this time, his earlier defeat. In the *Iliad* Achilles' death is a *donnée* of the poem, although not part of it. In book 9 he says that he has the power to choose between two destinies—either to die at Troy or, returning home, to live long and ingloriously. The *Iliad* itself is "about" this choice, and indeed about the angst and stress of all human choice: it is an existential poem. Achilles' decision to stay in Troy, and his awareness of what he has chosen, reverberate through the poem. His approaching death is unforgettably articulated in book 19 when the horse Xanthos speaks.

But Virgil reaffirms Turnus's affinity with the doomed Hector by stressing his ignorance of his own fate. He is prepared to take risks; he thinks he has a chance of victory until near the end of book 12. Homer's Hector, too, had acted with the impetuous, obstinate valour of a man who can't give up. He had expressed, as indeed also had Agamemnon, that tragic prescience of the city's destined fall which colours every reading of the poem, but of his own future he says only that no man can escape his destiny, and encourages his wife with cheerful words. When Turnus sets aside the plea of his despairing mother-in-law never to be, Amata, the implied reader will hear again the pleas of Priam and Hecuba

From *Virgil's Iliad: An Essay on Epic Narrative.* © 1984 by Cambridge University Press.

in *Iliad* 22, and, behind that, more faintly and distantly, the despairing foreboding of Andromache in book 6. Turnus calls Amata *mater*, thus emphasising the Homeric echo and adding pathos to a claimed relationship which, in his obstinate pride, he still clings to. The reader will also remember the countereffective divine protection exercised by Venus, which recalls, yet far outshines, the concern of Thetis for Achilles.

Virgil's Aeneas is a man set apart by a destiny of which he himself seems uncertain. Venus knows that her son will die and be deified within three years of the settlement of Latium, a tradition assumed for the implied reader. But Aeneas himself does not know this. His faith in his destiny is not based on any immense pride and self-regard (Achilles) nor on the soldier's assumption that either the bullet has your name on or it doesn't (Hector), but on a remote, bleak, awareness of a process of historical necessity wholly indifferent to the individual will. Even when a future beyond his personal fate is revealed to him, the future of the Roman nation (as the future doom of Troy was known to Agamemnon and Hector), he shows little understanding of it. In the Elysian fields he had wondered sadly how any human soul could bear to go through life's sorrows a second time, and his only question to Anchises, characteristically, concerned Marcellus, the young, flower-decked hero, untimely dead. And the magic Shield gives him pleasure as an artefact, but he cannot understand its significance.

For the reader of *Aeneid* 12, constructing as he reads a prefiguration of the Augustan settlement which lies outside Aeneas's grasp, there is an impatience, now, to reach the poem's end, to see Italian *uirtus*, for all its spectacular audacity and fire, yield to a stronger force, that of historical necessity, "what will be in the long run," that which awaits its time, the embodiment of Trojan *pietas* and patience in adversity. The qualities of toughness and endurance, of which Numanus had boasted that the Italians had the monopoly, was all the while building as the greatest strength of the Trojans: *durate*, Aeneas had said in his first words to his storm-wearied company in book 1: "endure."

Now the time has come, and in Turnus's angry and impetuous arming, the reader too feels a sense of urgency, or impatience for the poem's last dawn, when the duels between Paris and Menelaus, Hector and Achilles, will recur. But the killing of a rival suitor is also an Odyssean motif, and a distant memory of that other Homeric ending may come into a reading of *Aeneid* 12. In the scenes between Amata and Latinus domestic elements are as important as dynastic ones. The motif of *nostos*, homecoming, so strong in *Aeneid* 8 when Aeneas sailed up the Tiber to the site of Rome, is not wholly lost sight of.

The arming of Turnus is a full-scale epic episode based on several Iliadic exemplars, but postponed by Virgil until this last book, and now of much greater impact and significance than the very grand but display-conscious and, in terms of any military outcome, largely gestural arming of Agamemnon in *Iliad* 11; while the arming of Paris for his abortive duel with Menelaus in *Iliad* 3 strikes the reader almost as a kind of dressing-up. The other two Iliadic armings are those of Patroclus, full of pathos, and of Achilles, full of wrath, but also of foreboding, for it is on this occasion that the horse Xanthos prophesies his coming death. These two are the crucial armings of the *Iliad,* and it is these which carry for the implied reader of *Aeneid* 12 the strongest resonance. But the arming of Turnus is more decisive even than these, for it is the immediate prelude to the end of the war, and its true thematic function is to prefigure the battle of Actium. *Nunc . . . nunc tempus adest,* says Turnus, "now, now the time is at hand": that time of which the poet himself had warned, in book 10, when Turnus killed Pallas: *Turno tempus erit . . .* We are at a crisis and turning-point more significant than anything in the *Iliad*: it is time as *kairos* that is at hand, not time as *chronos.*

> For Turnus the time will come when he will pray for Pallas
> To be unharmed, give anything for that, and loathe
> This day, these spoils.

This is the time that has now come.

Aeneas's arming is no less powerfully presented:

> Nec minus interea maternis *saeuus* in armis.

> No less cruel he, in his mother's gift of arms.

Later, when the war breaks out again in defiance of the treaty, at the instigation of Juturna, Turnus's sister and Juno's agent (her name is a word-play on the other two names), Virgil tells how anger invades both armies and both leaders:

> non segnius ambo
> Aeneas Turnusque ruunt per proelia; nunc, nunc,
> fluctuat ira intus.

> with no less energy
> Aeneas and Turnus charge into battle. Now, now
> Is the surge of wrath.

That repeated *nunc, nunc,* picks up the *nunc, nunc, tempus adest* of Turnus's arming, words addressed to his own spear, perhaps echoing Mezentius's defiant *dextra mihi deus et telum* in book 10. In this last book we are taken back to book 7 and the first outbreak of war-madness in a structure of returning symmetry: the Virgilian Iliad ends as it began.

But the next day sees the treaty between Aeneas, still armed, still with the drawn sword, still *imperator,* and Latinus. Just before it is solemnised, Juno authorises Juturna to overthrow it, so that the reader follows the very grand and majestic account of the ritual with a kind of incredulity. The Homeric model is in *Iliad 3*—the treaty solemnised between Agamemnon and Priam before the duel between Menelaus and Paris. Aeneas's prayer at the treaty-making is a version of Agamemnon's: both invoke the Sun, the Earth, Zeus/Jupiter and the Rivers; both give undertakings about what they will do if they lose and if they win (in that order). Aeneas says that he thinks the latter more likely; Agamemnon does not actually say this, but he spends longer on what will happen if he wins than on what will happen if he loses. Virgil also assimilates the opening words of Aeneas's oath to a second oath of Agamemnon's, in the reconciliation between him and Achilles in book 19, when he swears that he has not touched Briseis. Just as that reconciliation is the prelude to Achilles' *aristeia,* and Hector's death, this one is a prelude to Aeneas's *aristeia* and Turnus's death.

With Latinus's oath Virgil introduces a new motif from the *Iliad,* one which contributes further to the sense of tension and unease generated by the scene between Juno and Juturna:

> By that same earth, Aeneas, sea and sky, I also swear
> And by the sun and moon and by two-headed Janus,
> And by the power of the infernal gods, and by the shrine of
> Dis.
> Hear this, o father of gods and men, who keepest treaties
> with the power of the thunderbolt.
> My hand on this altar, these sacred fires between us, and the
> gods, I so testify:
> Never shall come the day for the Italians to break this peace,
> this treaty,
> Whatsoever shall befall. No force shall bend my will,

While I have any power, no, not even if it should
Pour the whole world into the sea, the heavens into hell.
As this sceptre of mine (for he held his sceptre now)
Shall never again put forth leaves and give men shade
Once cut from the woods and its mother earth, trimmed by
    the knife,
Once a tree, now the hand of the artificer has decorated it
With bronze, to be borne by the elders of Latium.

Those last words are the words of Achilles' oath in the quarrel scene in *Iliad* 1, when he swears to Agamemnon that the time will come when he will be wanted in battle and will not be there. Achilles' threat comes true in the course of the story, just as Virgil's *Turno tempus erit* comes true when Turnus faces Aeneas wearing Pallas's baldric. Virgil has assimilated two aspects of Homer's Agamemnon. First, in relation to Priam, swearing a treaty before the duel between Helen's "suitors"; secondly, in relation to Achilles, both in the reconciliation between them in *Iliad* 19 and in the quarrel which set in motion the wrath theme. *Furor*, war-fury, stalks the plain of Latium as once it did the plain of Ilium. Virgil's Aeneas must not sulk, quarrel or withdraw: he must subsume the roles of Menelaus, rightful suitor, and Agamemnon, commander of the armies of victory, and assimilate these roles to those other roles, of Hector and Achilles: Hector to Turnus's Achilles, Achilles to his Hector. But the words of Achilles, the wrath-hero, are now adapted to Latinus, a figure in part of Priam, the old king, unable to control events.

Thus in the final scenes of the Virgilian Iliad, the implied reader must reconstruct the Homeric cause of that tragic death which alone could bring the absent champion back into battle and turn the tide of victory against the defenders. In the *Iliad* itself, the wrath theme is the preemptive narrative cause of the greater quarrel, between Achilles and Hector over Patroclus, itself a paradigm of the Trojan conflict as a whole. This final confrontation in *Iliad* 22 eclipsed the duel between Menelaus and Paris, so early in the poem, an expected ingredient of a Troy-tale but not causally linked to the wrath theme.

All these motifs and parallels, then, Virgil has blended into one: nowhere else is his extraordinary "esemplastic" power, to use Coleridge's remarkable word, so much in evidence. Wrath dominates *Aeneid* 12 but it is not the wrath only of Achilles dishonoured by Agamemnon, though that is alluded to in Latinus's oath, and though that quarrel, also over rivalry for a woman, reinforces the quarrel over Helen: the two stories parallel each other.

Latinus's oath is immediately nullified by the swift and sudden intervention of Juturna, which like that of Allecto in book 7 induces a fresh outburst of war fever. The throwing down of the altars, the defiling of the sacred vessels, the acts of sacrilege which follow the oath, are like the carnage in the *Iliad* which follows Zeus's promise to Thetis. Structurally, both oaths are followed by a renewal of fighting (there is no real fighting in the *Iliad* until book 4). It is to the situation, then, with which Homer's *Iliad* started that Virgil directs the reader as he reaches the twelfth book. The circle is almost complete.

It is at this point that one last crucial placing reference to the Trojan war is offered to the implied reader of *Aeneid* 12. We are taken back once more to the murals in the temple of Juno at Carthage in the first book: thus *Aeneid* 12 completes not only the circle of Homer's *Iliad* but the circle of the *Aeneid* itself, a complex double structure of ring-composition. Among the other murals Aeneas had seen Priam unarmed stretching forth his hands in supplication over Hector's corpse, *tendentemque manus Priamum conspexit inermem*. Now in book 12 when the war breaks out again in defiance of the solemn treaty Virgil writes

> At pius Aeneas dextram tendebat inermem.

Aeneas had been *pius* when he swore his oath, with drawn sword: that sword had become ceremonial; it awaited only Turnus. Now Aeneas is a second Priam, unarmed, suppliant, begging that the treaty be not dishonoured, in a deeply Roman appeal against wrath and on behalf of law:

> o cohibete iras! ictum iam foedus et omnes
> compositae leges.

> O control your wrath. Now is the treaty struck and all
> The laws enacted.

In his oath to Latinus Aeneas had already promised that the indigenous laws of Latium would remain in force even if the Trojans were victorious:

> paribus se legibus ambae
> inuictae gentes aeterna in foedera mittant.
> sacra deosque dabo; socer arma Latinus habeto
> imperium sollemne socer.

In equal laws let both
Nations undefeated make an everlasting covenant.
I shall set up our gods. Let my father-in-law Latinus hold
His ancient powers.

Latinus shall keep his *imperium*: the Roman concept of a duumvirate is strongly felt here, but in the defeat of Latinus after the breaking of the treaty the implied reader may also have to consider the kind of necessity whereby in defiance of all the proclaimed republican principles which stand against allowing all power to flow into one man's hands, Augustus himself nevertheless after Actium assumed all power and established the Principate. And Aeneas's religious mission—*sacra deosque dabo*—which was his sacred trust since he left Troy with the household gods and his father, symbols of *pietas* towards gods and men and the essential feature of the legend of Aeneas—becomes here a formulation of the powers of the head of state as *pontifex maximus*. In the final scene of the poem Aeneas must accept *imperium* and the role of lawgiver as well as *religio* and the role of *pontifex*. The breaking of the treaty has made this necessary. The Italians have shown themselves deficient in *pietas,* as did the Greeks when they sacked "the holy citadel of Priam": the denotative "holy" is that of a patriotic Greek poet, Homer himself, and if he was using a traditional formula that only confirms the persistence of the idea of Trojan *pietas*.

The spectacle of Aeneas stretching forth his unarmed hand in supplication against the sacrilege of treaty-breaking and the horror of war completes the cycle of the second Iliad. Aeneas must reenact the role of Priam before he reenacts that of Achilles, an Achilles whose wrath is that anger without which no man can fight at all. Sergeant-majors who incite their recruits to scream furiously at the dummies they run at with fixed bayonets act correctly in abnormal circumstances. To kill in cold blood is not in the nature of most men, and epic heroes are not psychopaths. Aeneas's *furor* is the direct outcome of war and is a direct response to it; Achilles' anger in *Iliad* 1 was a matter of personal pique over the spoils of war. Virgil's Iliad must enact a transcendence of the old heroic code of personal honour and material gain; Turnus must finally discredit that code, but so also must Aeneas himself. And perhaps what is to be discarded must first be discredited.

Nec minus interea maternis saeuus in armis
Aeneas acuit Martem et se suscitat ira.

> No less cruel he, in his mother's gift of arms,
> Whetted the knife of war and roused himself in wrath.

When the treaty was solemnised Aeneas laid aside his wrath; afterwards, that wrath reinvades him as much as it does Turnus:

> non segnius ambo
> Aeneas Turnusque ruunt per proelia; nunc, nunc
> fluctuat ira intus.

The allusion to Priam in the treaty-scene further enriches our reading of the final scenes of *Aeneid* 12 and deepens our understanding of what Virgil himself meant by the wrath of war. In *Aeneid* 2 Aeneas had described to Dido how Priam, before he was killed by Pyrrhus on that last dreadful night of Troy, said that even Achilles had not threatened him but was abashed, respected the rights due to old age and the suppliant, and had returned the body of Hector. The conduct of the Homeric Achilles in *Iliad* 24 provides the necessary and confirmed conclusion to the poem of his wrath. The chain of events which started with the quarrel in *Iliad* 1—Achilles' withdrawal, Zeus's promise to Thetis, the Trojan counterattack, Hector's *aristeia* and Patroclus's death, Achilles' reconciliation with Agamemnon, his *aristeia,* the revenge-killing of Hector and the dishonouring of his body—ends when Achilles, of his own free will, and not under divine coercion, though with strong divine prompting, surrenders Hector's dead body to Priam as, in book 1, he had refused to surrender Briseis's living body to Agamemnon.

But Aeneas, when he kills Turnus, is not only acting out again the Patroclus-motif: he must also avenge the murder of Priam. The wounding of Aeneas the suppliant is thus a crucial element in the poem's final scenes. It transfers to the Latins the guilt of the Greeks on the last night of Troy. They too have thrown down altars and overturned shrines, now they have tried to kill an unarmed man, *pontifex* not *imperator,* and only divine intervention heals the priest-king's wound. At the miracle of healing the surgeon Iapyx speaks some significant words. Once again, as in the *Iliad,* Aeneas is preserved for the future of his race.

> non haec humanis opibus, non arte magistra
> proueniunt, neque te, Aenea, mea dextera seruat:
> maior agit deus atque opera ad maiora remittit.

> No human help is here, and by no master's art
> Are these things done; not by my hand, Aeneas.
> A greater god acts here, to greater work sends you forth again.

The greater work which now awaits Aeneas will itself complete the *maius opus,* the greater work undertaken in *Aeneid* 7 by the implied author, of which book 12 is the fulfilment.

In the renewed conflict which now follows many more men are killed. The poet in his own person asks, stepping outside his own narrative, as he had at the start of book 1,

> tanton placuit concurrere motu,
> Iuppiter, aeterna gentis in pace futuras?

> Was this great conflict your will,
> Jupiter, between nations destined for eternal peace?

The implied reader recalls the eleventh line of the *Aeneid*: *tantaene animis caelestibus irae?,* "Is there in heavenly spirits so much wrath?" Jupiter had said in book 10 that the war between Latins and Trojans, indigenous and immigrant nations, civil war (*discordia*), was against his will (*abnueram*). He thus appeared to permit what he had not willed. This theological paradox persists throughout epic narrative. Men will their own acts, but within a pattern of destiny foreknown by the gods, resisted by some of them (Juno, Satan), and glimpsed by some mortals in moments of foreboding or revelation, by most men, never.

Virgil's questions are the beginning and end of the poem: "Is there in heavenly beings so much anger?" "Was this great conflict your will, Jupiter?" create a theological framework within the confines of which the narrative moves. But the questions—how can the gods permit, even encourage, world-evil—present the questioner in a role other than that of empathising narrator, and identify the poem's most significant "undecidability." If the *Aeneid* is a kind of pagan saint's legend, the reader must be expected to assent, as a believer, to the hero as a man operating in a universe in which historical necessity and divine providence move to their appointed end. If the poem is to be read as a poem of ideas, a spiritual pilgrimage for the reader as well as the hero, then the poet as metaphysician becomes more important in any construction of a total meaning for the poem than the epic narrator; the doubtful, speculative questions offer a morally ambiguous ideology which is bound to cast its shadow over any reading of the end of the poem. Indeed, if the reader is to assent to the implied author's ideological and moral uncertainty, it must alter his sense of the poem as a whole. The implied author has, after all, chosen to remind us of his opening question as we reach the poem's last narrative stretch. He need not have done this. The presented world of the poem must include this moral doubt, and the reader is included in that doubt. The gods do not merely allow men to enact history as Jupiter proclaimed in book 10. By their own discords, they create the tensions within which that history must be enacted.

The last question of the poet—"Was this great conflict your will, Jupiter?"—occurs in the poem's last invocation, itself cast in the form of a question.

> Quis mihi nunc tot acerba deus, quis carmine caedes
> diuersas obitumque ducum, quos aequore toto
> inque uicem nunc Turnus agit, nunc Troius heros,
> expediat?

> What god, now, I wonder, could unfold in song
> So many bitter things and diverse deaths and falls
> Of princes, over all the field
> By Turnus now despatched, now by the Trojan hero.

The invocation is a gesture towards Homeric authorial convention. Before long stretches of narrative, especially those containing many names, an appeal to the remembering Muses signals to the hearer a guarantee of the accuracy of the sequence and a correct attribution of the various achievements. It also implies that the poet himself is following tradition rather than composing in his own right. But Virgil uses the tradition quite differently. He implies the unwillingness, if not the powerlessness, of any god to assist in the chronicling of such bitter and tragic events. It is as if, the epic now moving to its end, the implied author is casting doubt on the epic tradition itself, with its divine apparatus, its aiding Muses, its never-failing machinery. It is not the historical but the moral credibility of the last events which seems beyond earthly chronicle and beyond divine inspiration. Could Jupiter himself underwrite so sad a story of the death of kings?

The paragraph beginning with this doubtful invocation, with its triple *nunc* (*now* who can tell what happened *now* . . .) ends with some lines already quoted:

> non segnius ambo
> Aeneas Turnusque ruunt per proelia; nunc, nunc
> fluctuat ira intus, rumpuntur nescia uinci
> pectora, nunc totis in uulnera uiribus itur.

The two heroes are compared to forest fires converging on dry brushwood, and to mountain rivers. They are alike in their destructive power, in their violence, in their lack of control. The whole emphasis of the paragraph is on the indistinguishable conduct of the two sides and the two leaders. The triple *nunc* at the end of the passage encloses it inside a narrative "present" which, in the poet's own "now," is total and inescapable. The elemental blindness of irrationality is like fire and water. In natural disaster there is only a timeless "now." So in the double *aristeia* of the two heroes: often the reader cannot quickly identify the killer, either by the *hic* or *ille* which designates him, or by the undifferentiated catalogue of victims, most of whom simultaneously enter and leave the poem, like names on a list of the fallen. I believe we can see here an authorial intention which has not been fully recognised. Servius was the first to notice a confusion, but suppose it to be deliberate? Suppose the implied author to be saying that total war cannot be contained within decorous epic conventions? Suppose that, ultimately, it does not matter who kills whom? Suppose that, like Jupiter, the poet makes no distinction between the two sides? On such hypotheses a view of war emerges which is closer to that of Wilfred Owen than to Homer: that emphasis on *nunc* does not allow the implied reader to pretend that this all belongs in the remote past.

> If you could hear, at every jolt, the blood
> Come gargling from the froth-corrupted lungs
>
> . . . .
>
> My friend, you would not tell with such high zest
> To children ardent for some desperate glory
> The old Lie: Dulce et decorum est
> Pro patria mori.
> [Wilfred Owen, "Dulce et Decorum Est"]

But there is one victim of *furor* who stands out in these final scenes. Though briefly narrated, and without direct speech, the suicide of Amata is crucial to Turnus's final isolation. Moreover, there are uneasy echoes of another queen's suicide. Now both leaders have this on their conscience; once more, the scales are balanced, *Tros Rutulusne fuat, nullo discrimine habebo*: Jupiter's words come grimly home again to the reader. Both queens die, what is more, as a direct result of thwarted dynastic ambition.

Just as in book 10 Jupiter abandoned the war to the heroes who must fight it, who must enact history, so now he abandons Turnus, or Turnus thinks he does. Amata, too, had killed herself under a delusion, that Turnus was already dead. And perhaps he is, as good as dead: *di me terrent et Iuppiter hostis,* he says; "the gods terrify me, Jupiter himself is my enemy." He sees that he has crossed the permitted bounds of his power, into an isolation comparable, perhaps, in its pagan context with the isolation of Marlowe's Dr Faustus. Turnus in the closing scene of the epic retains the bravado which has been his most conspicuous characteristic, but the despair of those six words (he speaks after that only once more, to surrender to Aeneas and ask that his body be returned for burial, in the conventional and formal manner of the old-style Homeric hero) is absolute. It is a despair already articulated by his sister Juturna, who, lamenting her immortality, asks

> Could any abyss of the earth be deep enough
> To open and swallow me and send me to the shades?

Turnus himself had used some of those same "Faustian" words in his soliloquy in book 10 when he was carried away on the ship in his vain pursuit of the phantom Aeneas: but only some of them. He had not then fully experienced the longing to die now articulated by Juturna. In this growing atmosphere of despair Virgil more and more reminds the reader of parallels between Turnus and Dido. And because there is a parallel with Dido there is also one with another suicide of an enemy of Rome, Cleopatra, and thus Aeneas in his hour of victory will complete his prefiguration of Augustus at Actium and, with whatever reluctance or show of reluctance, accept supreme power. The single combat was not only a device to spare more lives; it was a means of ensuring that the survivor was without a challenger and could now proceed to dispose as he wished the total power which had come to him, by the will of the gods.

There is a strong sense in any reading of the poem nowadays, and this has perhaps been true ever since the Renaissance, that Turnus and Dido are tragic victims in the classical mode, hubristic, flawed by *hamartia,* proclaiming a self-deluding innocence. Turnus' farewell reads like an operatic aria, as indeed does Dido's, with its final dramatic gesture, *sic, sic iuuat ire sub umbras,* as she stabs herself on the words *sic, sic.* Turnus too makes a self-dramatising and self-justifying statement:

> uos, o mihi Manes
> este boni, quoniam superis auersa uoluntas.
> sancta ad uos anima atque istius inscia culpae
> descendam magnorum haud umquam indignus auorum.

> O shades below, to me
> Be good, now that heaven's will has turned from me
> I shall to you a holy soul and innocent of blame
> Go down for ever worthy of my great forefathers.

Turnus proclaims his innocence, not as a general moral claim, but as a specific repudiation of the one fault no hero can carry: cowardice. It is an act of bravado, or propitiation to the gods of the underworld, *dis manibus,* and perhaps a belated defence against Drances' rankling accusations in book 11. Turnus has always put himself first, and does so to the end: again, he acts like a pagan Faustus, and the reader may now perhaps also recall Juno's defiance of the Olympian will: "if I can't persuade the gods above, I'll stir up hell." Aeneas has never put himself first, he has acted throughout *non sponte sua,* as Augustus also claimed he acted, not by his own will but by that of the people of Italy who asked him to be their leader. Dido had put her own political and sexual needs first; so did Cleopatra. The end for which Aeneas has laboured is not merely outside himself: it lies beyond his son's lifetime, in remote centuries which will only start to evolve with Romulus. Only beyond two myths can Roman history begin. That end lies, too, beyond the poem as narrative, yet it is an essential part of any reading of it, since the reader is not meant to be bound by Aeneas's perspectives, but to see beyond them. And how is the reader to be stopped from seeing also beyond Virgil's?

Yet the grandeur of Turnus's egotism, in his daring to cross the permitted limits of his world, the courage which shines through his egotism, will not vanish wholly from history, and (like Faustus's soul) "ne'er be found." It will persist in many acts of personal *uirtus* in time of danger throughout Rome's history, acts depicted on Aeneas's Shield, associated with Romulus, Horatius Cocles, Cloelia (of whom Camilla is the type), Manlius, Cato. Turnus's grandeur dominates book 12 as Dido's had dominated book 4.

The settlement between Jupiter and Juno in book 12 is a mirror of the scene between Jupiter and Venus in book 1: a mighty instance of returning symmetry or "ring-composition." The smile with which Jupiter turns to Juno

olli subridens hominum rerumque repertor

mirrors the smile with which he had reassured Venus in book 1 that all in the long run should be well olli subridens hominum sator atque deorum.

The words are a clear signal from the implied author that the reader is approaching the end.

> This nation which shall arise from Italian stock
> Shall in its piety transcend both men and gods.
> You shall see it.
> And no nation shall honour you as they shall.

Here is the famous transformation of Juno from inveterate anti-Trojan to guardian of Rome, a member, with Minerva and Jupiter himself, of the "Capitoline triad" of deities who symbolised *imperium sine fine*. "You can't beat us—join us": *uidebis,* "you shall see it," is a joke of the implied author (and part of the joke is that he speaks now with the voice of Jupiter) to the Augustan reader. Not *uidebis* but *uides*. The future becomes present and completes a meaning. Not "the meaning": for the modern reader cannot make that particular syntactical change. For him, the implied future is already past. Yet he may, reaching this end, suspend syntax, with that future not yet mediated into history, "something evermore about to be," held in a past remoter from him than Troy was from the Augustans.

The end of the *Aeneid* is not "just" the death of Turnus, abrupt, perfunctory even, with its repeated curtain line already used for Camilla as Homer had used Patroclus's for Hector. Homer saw that Hector's death could not be the end of the *Iliad*; there had to be a resolution of the wrath theme, the long decrescendo of the games and the ransoming of Hector's body to Priam, alone in the tent with his son's killer.

The *Aeneid* has two endings. The sending of Turnus's soul is the narrator's last task, the god's last sad act of chronicle vicariously and reluctantly performed.

> What god now, I wonder, could unfold in song
> So many bitter things and diverse deaths and falls
> Of princes, over all the field
> By Turnus now despatched, now by the Trojan hero.

When Aeneas despatches Turnus, the reader's task may seem to be at an end. The narrative is complete, the presented world of the Virgilian Iliad stops, with the death of Turnus as Hector and the triumph of Aeneas as Achilles. But the reader must also transform the narrative by including the process by which the presented world is offered, and make this a part of his understanding of the poem's total meaning. And for this there is the poem's other ending to be included: that is, the scene between Jupiter and Juno, and, behind that, the mirror scene between Jupiter and Venus, so that in a sense the poem's "end" was written in book 1. When the reader gets to the end of book 12, images and motifs from book 1 remain in, or return to, his mind, a persistence more powerful than, and in a sense transcending, any specific reading: almost an independent life in the memory of the poem's meaning, a life independent, that is, of the actual "text." We may emphasise different parts of the poem with each reading, select this, exclude that, but our interaction with the poem will in the end be more than the sum of any particular passages read or translated, and will lead to the construction of an *Aeneid sine fine,* "without end," the poem as a prelude to history and to the understanding of history.

Patterns of returning symmetry are found in a variety of narrative fictions from Homer onwards. For the reader of long works, these structures facilitate the construction of a total meaning: the sense of the ending involves a memory of the beginning: the true significance of the presented world of the fiction is perceived through the presentational process itself. When we first met Aeneas in *Aeneid* 1, he was cold, tired, frightened and wishing he had died at Troy. "His limbs were numb with cold," *soluuntur frigore membra* (1.92): the allusion here, and in the speech which follows, the *o terque quaterque beati,* "o thrice and four times blessed," is to *Odyssey* 5, where Odysseus is also lost in a storm and far from the goal of his *nostos.* Odysseus wished he had died when the Trojans tried so hard to get him after Achilles' death. Aeneas wishes he had not survived Diomede's onslaught, and had died alongside Sarpedon and Hector, deaths closely linked with the saga of Achilles' wrath, deaths fated to be reenacted in the Italian Iliad. Those words far away in book 1, *soluuntur frigore membra,* recur in the last line but one of book 12: now they describe Turnus, and the cold is not that of the elements, or of a wished for and elusive death, but of the thing itself, inescapably there. In 1.97 Aeneas wished he had died at the right hand of Diomede, "I wish I could have poured out this soul of mine": at the end of book 12 it is Aeneas's right hand which pours out Turnus's soul. The motif of Aeneas's preservation for posterity, first heard at the poem's outset, is heard again at its ending. It is for this he was spared. He has reenacted the Iliadic vendetta, not just to avenge a personal loss (the Pallas-Patroclus motif) but to secure the future "so that the race of Dardanus might not perish," thus validating both Iliadic and Roman prophecy.

At the end of the *Aeneid,* Aeneas is nearly persuaded into an act of mercy which, had he managed it, would have perhaps changed the modern reader's sense of the entire text.

> et iam iamque magis cunctantem flectere sermo
> coeperat.

> And now he hesitated, now Turnus's words nearly
> Turned him from his purpose.

But the Iliadic motif of the armour of Patroclus is introduced, and Aeneas plunges in the sword, in a last access of that *furor* which in Homer's Achilles was by the last book of the *Iliad* spent: that same *furor* which Hercules, the type of culture hero and saviour hero, had shown in his killing of Cacus in book 8, itself prefigurative of this last duel. Hercules in book 8 is *furens animis,* he is *feruidus ira.* This is the model for Aeneas at the end of book 12, *furiis accensus et ira / terribilis.* When he puts in the sword he is *feruidus,* in contrast to Turnus, on whom the cold of death has settled:

> "Pallas te hoc uulnere, Pallas
> immolat et poenam scelerato ex sanguine sumit."
> hoc dicens ferrum aduerso sub pectore condit
> feruidus; ast illi soluuntur frigore membra
> uitaque cum gemitu fugit indignata sub umbras.

> "Pallas strikes you down, with this cut Pallas
> Takes this vengeance, sheds your evil blood."
> Thus saying he buries his sword in the other's breast
> In the heat of the moment. But the other's limbs are cold,
> And his reluctant spirit, crying, vanishes to the dead.

Structurally, the Iliadic revenge motif becomes a cover for the politically necessary elimination of a dangerous rival. (So too for Octavian the morally outrageous conduct of Antony with Cleopatra provided a cover for what was politically necessary.) At the end of the *Odyssey* no reader wants Odysseus to spare the suitors, and perhaps Virgil wanted his implied reader to take some of his sense of the ending of the *Aeneid* from the end of the *Odyssey.* But there is no psychological paradigm, and, for the modern, though perhaps not the implied Augustan reader, only a doubtful moral one. Despite the oracles, it is hard for the reader to feel much enthusiasm for Aeneas's claim to Lavinia or to see Turnus in the role of Paris rather than Menelaus. But for the implied reader

Aeneas is Menelaus, who has traversed the sea to claim his lawful bride and secure the succession. The pattern of arrival, combat and victory (for the absence of Achilles is the crucial single element in the plot of the *Iliad*) seems peculiarly Homeric, and is common to both *Iliad* and *Odyssey*. Behind the despatching to the shades of Turnus's reluctant soul it is not easy, though, to detect the twittering shades of Penelope's suitors, down in Hades among the souls of Troy's greatest dead. It is to these great warrior ghosts that Turnus, in his self-proclaiming pride, descends.

Epic heroes may make the world a better place, albeit only for the time being. They cannot make it a good one. For Virgil all war is mad and one cannot conduct oneself morally on the battlefield. Only in an Odyssean sense can the killing of Turnus be morally acceptable, and then only if we import into our reading a sense that Aeneas's marriage to Lavinia was made in heaven long before her earthly betrothal to Turnus. This is a revenge killing, for Pallas-Patroclus; and for the killing in the *Iliad* of Trojan Hector, so that the reader may transfer to the furious Aeneas some of the anger he, the reader of the *Iliad* also, felt at the treatment of Hector by the furious Achilles. The foul deeds which Homer himself says Achilles devised for noble Hector are now requited.

Homer's Trojan war was fought for a domestic cause, yet clearly the deaths of so many great heroes and the ultimate destruction of the city of Troy, distantly descried within the poem yet lying, as an event, beyond it, gives the work a tragic grandeur and plenitude which transcends the story of Helen: transcends also the wrath theme. Virgil's Lavinia is much more of a minor character than the Helen of *Iliad* 3, whom we see relating in such different ways to Priam, Aphrodite and Paris (let alone the Helen of *Odyssey* 4, reunited with Menelaus): indeed, Lavinia never speaks. It is not because of her that Aeneas is seized with that last cold fit of wrath. Turnus had not expected to be spared: he faced his destiny to the end. His request for decent burial follows that of Hector to Achilles. Aeneas does not echo Achilles' terrible rejection of that plea. Indeed, he goes much further than merely not rejecting the plea for burial: he nearly spared his life, *dextramque repressit*, "stayed his hand." Some critics have suggested that the final decision was a piece of covert political allegory, an encoded reference to acts of cruelty by Augustus against political rivals. But I know of no evidence for this. In *The Faerie Queene* Spenser has left the reader signs by which to construct from the narrative of Mercilla and Duessa an allegorical "meaning" in terms of contemporary politics. There seems nothing comparable in the final scene of the *Aeneid*. What ought to surprise the reader, or so it seems to me, is not that Aeneas does not spare Turnus, but that he should have hesitated at all. The hesitation constitutes the surprise.

We know that Virgil abandoned the idea of an epic about Augustus in favour of a different kind of epic, a kind of synchronisation of the *Iliad* and Actium. The Homeric epics remain the principal ordering structure of the *Aeneid*. But this does not enclose readings of the poem within the confines, large and complex though they are, of the Homeric epics. It is unfortunate that some modern readings of the *Aeneid* take the poem's political and historical signs as propaganda, and there is sometimes a tendency to suppress these and see the poem "without" or "despite" this element. Or it is argued that Virgil himself lost faith in the Augustan dream, and wanted the poem destroyed not just because it had not been finally revised but because of some fancied "philosophical" revulsion from *Realpolitik*; and that Augustus's determination to have it published posthumously was a propagandist decision.

Augustus did not need propaganda. He had after Actium no rival, but what he did want was display, in various forms, in sculpture as well as poetry, of the values and virtues of the principate. Jupiter's first speech, for example, may be read like that. The benefits to Rome of the new regime flowed from the *princeps* downwards in a great expression of celebration. Virgil saw in the popular story of Aeneas a paradigm of those benefits, the story of the assumption, with some appropriate show of cautious reluctance, by one man of powers traditionally and destructively divided.

Virgil began his poetic career, in the first *Eclogue,* with an idealistic *Dankgesang* for the benefits, in *otium* and *libertas,* of the new leader, a saviour-hero for whom, as for Hercules, extravagantly figurative language was appropriate both in terms of literary tradition and as a political gesture. Between the pastoral poet's heartfelt thanksgiving for peace to write—*deus nobis haec otia fecit,* "a god has made us this peace"—and the vision of the *pax Augusta* in Jupiter's speech, in *Aeneid* 1, it is hard to register any falling-off of enthusiasm for the new order.

At the end of the *Odyssey,* Homer fulfilled, in another returning symmetry, the promise of Zeus to his daughter Athene in book 1: Odysseus, a good man, who took heed of the gods, would come safe home, unlike Agamemnon, and despite the opposition of Poseidon. (The fulfilment of a divine promise thus provides the starting-point for Homer's two epics.) This structure is repeated in the *Aeneid*: Aeneas, a good man, made safe landfall, as promised by Jupiter to his daughter in book 1, propitiated Juno and secured the Trojan succession by dynastic inter-marriage. If Aeneas had not hesitated, there would be no problem at the end of the poem.

But he did. Would the implied reader, should he, have hesitated also, delaying assent to the final slaughter, the last piece of the Homeric jigsaw? It is an assent the modern reader, such is the nature of the poem, may continue to withhold. He may indeed want to "lose" the poem after that *iam iamque magis*; to emphasise that moment, prolonged as though for ever, and skip the final act with its double Homeric allusion to Hector and the suitors ("noble Hector" and the suitors, more deplorable than Turnus). The combined tragic and moral strengths of the *Iliad* and the *Odyssey* could not provide Virgil with any other ending for his unendable poem. Where else could he have got another ending?

There was nowhere else. Aeneas's last act is an existential choice, terrible as such choices are; so it was also for the implied author, self-obliged to reenact Homer in a historical context which lets in the reader's own doubts and insecurities.

Among all the burdens Aeneas carried—his father and his gods from Homeric Troy, the Shield bearing the fame and destiny of the future Rome—itself a model of the universe, which Atlas bore on his shoulders and which Hercules traversed in the cause of civilisation—the burden of Homeric epic was the greatest, for it was the poet's own. In the last lines of the poem he all but lays it aside—but not quite. The hero who turns his sword in Turnus's heart is the same man of whom, far back in book 1, Virgil wrote: fate-driven, pursued by divine hatred, bur-dened, unlucky. His last words to his son in book 12 are important now:

> Learn virtue and the truth about a hero's labours
> From me. But luck? Get that from others.

Of all Aeneas's burdens, this last killing is the heaviest, yet it always awaited him. The time that was foretold for Turnus was also his time, his *kairos*. He could not know, till the moment came, the doubts and hesitations it would involve. The hesitation at the end is the hero's and the reader's, for an existential choice is made for all, and sets a certain stamp upon humanity.

And perhaps that hesitation is also the poet's. His sense of having left the *Aeneid* unrevised, of being unable to complete a fully achieved text, are well authenticated. Thus there entered into the poem when it was published with its fifty-seven hemistichs (some of them editorially completed, though these completions have never entered the text), a sense of the finally unachieved.

Thus any reading of the poem will, even more than would be the case with a fully achieved work (for no finality is conceivable in any act of reading) produce a sense of having reached only one of many possible meanings. (*The Faerie Queene,* not merely unrevised but incomplete in terms of the poet's own published schema, is a more extreme example.) The very abruptness and, in a curious sense, the very finality of the ending of the *Aeneid* leaves the reader with a sense of uncertainty. The ending was foreseen and structurally "given," and indeed in the scene on Olympus the reader has already gone past, overshot that narrative "end": in its vaster perspective the death of Turnus seems almost like a flashback, although written in the historic present, "narrative time." Yet because the devices of prophecy had opened the poem up beyond its narrative end, the reader may wonder about the possibility of ending at all an epic whose revealed theme was *imperium sine fine.* And does not the uneasy "end" imply for the modern reader doubts and ironies about *imperium sine fine* which, once read into the poem, seem to become Virgil's own? The splendours which the poem "prophetically" opens up are now part of a past which for many readers exists now chiefly *in* the poem itself. The author and his implied (Augustan) reader had access to external referents, institutions, monuments, the living tissue of history, which he drew upon in the great visions of Rome in books 1, 6 and 8. Now those descriptions often amount to all, or nearly all, we have. The rest has gone, or survives in material only the specialist can interpret. They have been superseded in our minds by a past Virgil could not imagine. Any reading of the *Aeneid,* then, will be coloured by insights and images to which Virgil had no access. And this too, in some unmistakable way, becomes part of the poem. The old idea of Virgil as *anima naturaliter Christiana,* poised uncertainly at the very end of the era of what Dante called the false and lying gods, unable to escape from the pagan world to whose values he seemed not wholly to assent, remains powerful. And we may recall other words of Dante, from the *Purgatorio,* the last words he wrote for Virgil to say in *his* epic:

> Expect no more signs from me
>
> . . . .
>
> You are free to choose.

I believe the peace and freedom, *otium* and *libertas,* with which Virgil hailed the Augustan settlement, remained for him the cornerstone of his creative career. I believe that in writing the *Aeneid,* his greatest work, and especially in writing the second half of it, *maius opus,* he found himself less free in his choices. As he went on, he created more and more signs to denote a hero for whom there simply did not exist enough freedom of choice. Dante perceived with love and reverence how close Virgil might have come to understanding the nature and value of freedom in choice and action. When he made Jupiter in book 10 detach himself from the action, he gave his heroes as much freedom as it was in his power to give them. The modern reader may invest Aeneas with a greater range of insight and choice than he could have possessed for his creator, and may also create an implied author with access to value-systems which lie in fact beyond the limits of the poem and of the pagan world. Yet the reader, importing these, is not, save in the narrowest and most scholastic sense, "misinterpreting" the *Aeneid.* Indeed, he may be uncovering a more significant text, one that may be related to a greater range of insights into history and humanity.

Chronology

B.C. 70	Publius Vergilius Maro born on October 5, near Mantua.
ca.60–54	Virgil is educated in Cremona. After he finishes studies in 54, Virgil goes to Milan. During this time, the First Triumvirate (Caesar, Pompey, and Crassus) is formed, and Caesar begins his Gallic wars.
53	Virgil moves to Rome, to begin legal training.
49	Having turned from his study of the law, Virgil is probably living and writing poetry in an Epicurean society in Cumae. Caesar crosses the Rubicon, thus initiating civil war against Pompey (Crassus has already been killed).
44	The Ides of March—Caesar assassinated on the steps of the Capitol, thus fomenting further civil war, this time between the Second Triumvirate (Octavian, Antony, and Lepidus) and Brutus and Cassius, Caesar's killers.
42	Defeat of Brutus and Cassius at the Battle of Philippi.
41	Virgil begins work on *Eclogues*. Further civil war—Antony against Octavian.
38	Virgil completes *Eclogues* and begins *Georgics*.
37	Virgil publishes *Eclogues*.
31	Having completed *Georgics*, Virgil begins work on the *Aeneid*. Battle of Actium—Octavian defeats Antony and Cleopatra.
29	Virgil publishes *Georgics*.
27	Octavian now known by the title Augustus.
23	Marcellus, nephew to Augustus, dies; reference to him in *Aeneid*, book 6.
19	Virgil sails to Greece to revise *Aeneid*, which he thinks will take about three years. Augustus urges him to return to Italy, which he does, falling ill on the voyage. On his death-

bed in Brindisi, Virgil insists that the manuscript of the *Aeneid* be burned after his death, as it is incomplete. He dies in Brindisi on September 21. Augustus overrules Virgil's request; and the *Aeneid* is published after only minimal revision by Virgil's executors.

Contributors

HAROLD BLOOM, Sterling Professor of the Humanities at Yale University, is the author of *The Anxiety of Influence, Poetry and Repression,* and many other volumes of literary criticism. His forthcoming study, *Freud: Transference and Authority,* attempts a full-scale reading of all of Freud's major writings. A MacArthur Prize Fellow, he is general editor of five series of literary criticism published by Chelsea House.

VIKTOR PÖSCHL is best known for his landmark studies on Cicero and Virgil. He is the author of *The Art of Vergil.*

THOMAS GREENE is the Frederick Clifford Ford Professor of English and Comparative Literature at Yale University. His books include *The Light in Troy, The Descent from Heaven,* and a study of Rabelais.

ADAM PARRY was Professor of Classics at Yale. His tragic early death prevented a full harvest of his gifts, but his essays on Greek and Latin poetry, and his edition of the writings of his father, Milman Parry, are lasting contributions.

W. R. JOHNSON teaches in the Department of Classics at Cornell University and is the author of *Darkness Visible: A Study of Vergil's* Aeneid.

BARBARA J. BONO is Assistant Professor of English at the State University of New York at Buffalo. She is author of *Literary Transvaluation: From Vergilian Epic to Shakespearean Tragicomedy.*

K. W. GRANSDEN teaches at the University of Warwick and is the author of *Virgil's Iliad: An Essay on Epic Narrative.*

Bibliography

Arethusa 14, no. 1 (1981). Special Virgil issue.

Auden, W. H. "Secondary Epic." In *Homage to Clio,* reprinted in *W. H. Auden: Collected Poems,* edited by Edward Mendelson. New York: Random House, 1976.

Auerbach, Erich. *Mimesis: The Representation of Reality in Western Literature.* New York: Doubleday, 1957.

Broch, Hermann. *The Death of Virgil.* Translated by Jean Starr Untermeyer. New York: Pantheon, 1945.

Burke, Paul F., Jr. "The Role of Mezentius in the *Aeneid.*" *The Classical Journal* 69, no. 3 (1974): 202–7.

Camps, W. A. *An Introduction to Virgil's* Aeneid. Oxford: Oxford University Press, 1969.

Clausen, Wendell. "An Interpretation of the *Aeneid.*" *Harvard Studies in Classical Philology* 68 (1964): 139–47.

Commager, Steele, ed. *Virgil: A Collection of Critical Essays.* Englewood Cliffs, N.J.: Prentice-Hall, 1966.

Culler, Jonathan. "Apostrophe." *Diacritics* 7, no. 4 (1977): 159–69.

Di Cesare, Mario A. *The Altar and the City: A Reading of Vergil's* Aeneid. New York: Columbia University Press, 1974.

Duckworth, G. E. "The Significance of Nisus and Euryalus for *Aeneid* 9–12." *American Journal of Philology* 88 (1967): 129–50.

—————. *Structural Patterns and Proportions in Vergil's* Aeneid. Ann Arbor: University of Michigan Press, 1962.

Eliot, T. S. *On Poets and Poetry.* New York: Farrar, Straus, 1957.

Graves, Robert. "The Virgil Cult." *Virginia Quarterly Review* 38 (1962): 13–35.

Highet, Gilbert. *Poets in a Landscape.* London: Hamish Hamilton, 1957.

Horsfall, Nicholas. "Numanus Remulus: Ethnography and Propaganda in *Aen.* ix. 598ff." *Latomus* 30 (1971): 1108–16.

Jackson Knight, W. F. *Roman Vergil.* 2d ed. London: Faber & Faber, 1966.

Lewis, R. W. B. "Homer and Virgil: The Double Themes." *Furioso* 5, no. 2 (1950): 47–59.

Little, D. A. "The Death of Turnus and the Pessimism of the *Aeneid.*" *Australian Universities Modern Language Association Journal* 33 (1970): 67–76.

Mack, Sara. *Patterns of Time in Virgil.* Hamden, Conn.: Archon, 1978.

Montagu, John R. C., ed. *Cicero and Virgil: Studies in Honour of Harold Hunt*. Amsterdam: Adolf M. Hakkert, 1972.

Moskalew, Walter. *Formular Language and Poetic Design in the* Aeneid. *Mnemosyne*, suppl. vol. 73 (1982).

Nisbet, Robert. *History of the Idea of Progress*. New York: Basic Books, 1980.

Otis, Brooks. *Virgil: A Study in Civilized Poetry*. Oxford: Clarendon, 1963.

————. "Virgilian Narrative in the Light of Its Precursors and Successors." *Studies in Philology* 73 (1976): 1–28.

Putnam, Michael C. J. "*Aeneid* VII and the *Aeneid*." *American Journal of Philology* 91, no. 4 (1970): 408–30.

————. *The Poetry of the* Aeneid. Cambridge: Harvard University Press, 1965.

Quinn, Kenneth. *Virgil's* Aeneid: *A Critical Description*. Ann Arbor: University of Michigan Press, 1968.

Reed, Nicholas. "The Gates of Sleep in *Aeneid* 6." *Classical Quarterly* 23 (1973): 311–15.

Segal, C. P. "*Aeternum per saecula nomen:* The Golden Bough and the Tragedy of History." Part 1, *Arion* 4 (1965): 617–57; part 2, *Arion* 5 (1966): 34–72.

Thornton, Agathe. *The Living Universe: Gods and Men in Virgil's* Aeneid. Dunedin: University of Otago Press, 1976.

West, D., and T. Woodman, eds. *Creative Imitation and Latin Literature*. Cambridge: Cambridge University Press, 1980.

Willcock, M. M. "Battle Scenes in the *Aeneid*." *Proceedings of the Cambridge Philological Society* n.s. 29 (1983): 87–99.

Williams, Gordon. *Change and Decline: Roman Literature in the Early Empire*. Berkeley: University of California Press, 1978.

————. *Technique and Ideas in the* Aeneid. New Haven: Yale University Press, 1983.

————. *Tradition and Originality in Roman Poetry*. Oxford: Clarendon, 1968.

Williams, R. D. "The Purpose of the *Aeneid*." *Antichthon* 1 (1967): 29–41.

————. *Virgil: Greece and Rome*. Oxford: Clarendon, 1967.

Wilson, C. H. "Jupiter and the Fates in the *Aeneid*." *Classical Quarterly* 29 (1979): 361–71.

Acknowledgments

"Aeneas" by Viktor Pöschl from *The Art of Vergil: Image and Symbol in the Aeneid* by Viktor Pöschl, © 1962 by the University of Michigan. Reprinted by permission of the University of Michigan Press.

"Virgil's Style" (originally entitled "Virgil") by Thomas Greene from *The Descent from Heaven: A Study in Epic Continuity* by Thomas Greene, © 1963 by Thomas Greene. Reprinted by permission of the author and Yale University Press.

"The Two Voices of Virgil's *Aeneid*" by Adam Parry from *Arion* 2, no. 4 (Winter 1963), © 1963 by the Trustees of Boston University. Reprinted by permission.

"Depths and Surfaces" (originally entitled "Varia Confusus Imagine Rerum: Depths and Surfaces") by W. R. Johnson from *Darkness Visible: A Study of Vergil's* Aeneid by W. R. Johnson, © 1976 by the Regents of the University of California. Reprinted by permission of the University of California Press.

"The Dido Episode" (originally entitled "Vergil's Dido and Aeneas: Tensions and Transformations") by Barbara J. Bono from *Literary Transvaluation: From Vergilian Epic to Shakespearean Tragicomedy* by Barbara J. Bono, © 1984 by the Regents of the University of California. Reprinted by permission of the University of California Press.

"War and Peace" by K. W. Gransden from *Virgil's Iliad: An Essay on Epic Narrative* by K. W. Gransden, © 1984 by Cambridge University Press. Reprinted by permission.

Index

Achilles: Aeneas compared to, 133; death of, 127; and Hector, 127–28; oath of, 131

Actium (battle): Aeneas's actions at, 65; significance of, 138. *See also* Battle of Actium

Aeneas: Achilles compared to, 133; at Actium, 65; as antihero, 118–19; Mark Antony and, 65, 70–71; arming of, 129; and Ascanius, 27; as Asiatic, 29–30; and Atlas, 40; Augustus compared to, 64–65, 70–71, 138, 139; bitterness of, 46; burdens of, 145–46; as cad, 42, 69–70; in Carthage, 120; character of, 15–17, 27–28, 42–43, 45; as Christian hero, 24–25; as Christian ideal, 4–5; cloak of, 40; compassion of, 17–18, 22–23, 100–101, 106; concern with descendants of, 12; concern with destiny of, 64–65, 128; critical views of, 1; death images of, 67; delusions of, 101; and Dido, 16–17, 19–20, 40, 70, 103, 106–12, 115, 116–17, 122–23; doom of, 27, 82–83; and duty, sense of, 13–14; emotional depth of, 42–43; energy of, 46; epic identity of, 64–65; exile as motif of, 10–11; as failed hero, 68–70, 73; faith of, 44–45; and family, 120; and fate, 66, 68; firmness of, 20–21; and future, visions of, 120; generosity of, 32–33; gods as viewed by, 114; and grief, 72–73; as head of state, 133; and Hector, 11, 127–28; Hellenus and, 68; heroism of, 24, 27–28; as historic commentary, 61, 71; historical consciousness of, 13–14; historic identifications of, 64–65; as historical prelude, 141; Homeric heroes and, 62–63; humanitas and, 17, 27–28; and Iarbus, 34–35; identity of, 47–48; *Iliad* compared to, 141; inner pilgrimage of, 29–30; as interpreter of events, 104–5; and Juno, 103–4; and Jupiter, 34–38; *lacrimas inanes* of, 18–20; Latin leaders against, 57; and Lausus, 99–100; *magnitudo animi* of, 14–15; mission of, 124; moral goals of, 25; nobility of, 43; and oak simile, 18–19; oath as prelude to *aristeia,* 130; Odysseus compared to, 9–10, 70; and pain, attitude toward, 25–26; and Palinurus, death of, 20–21; Pallas and, 21–22; past and, 12, 105, 109; patriotism and, 99–100; *pietas* and, 14–15; preservation of,